The Algarve

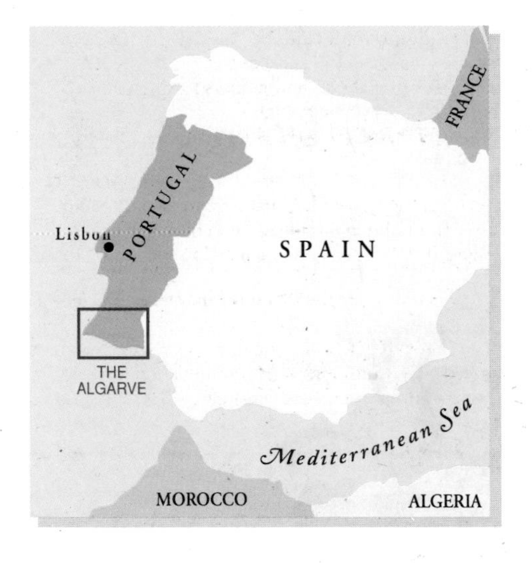

HarperCollins*Publishers*

YOUR COLLINS TRAVELLER

Your Collins Traveller Guide will help you find your way around your chosen destination quickly and easily. It is colour-coded for easy reference:

The blue section answers the question 'I would like to see or do something; where do I go and what do I see when I get there?' This section is arranged as an alphabetical list of topics and it is recommended that an up-to-date atlas or street plan is used in conjunction with their location maps. Within each topic you will find:

- A selection of the best examples on offer.
- How to get there, costs and opening hours for each entry.
- The outstanding features of each entry.
- A simplified map, with each entry plotted and the nearest landmark or transport access.

The red section is a lively and informative gazetteer. It offers:

- Essential facts about the main places and cultural items. What is La Bastille? Who was Michelangelo? Where is Delphi?

The gold section is full of practical and invaluable travel information. It offers:

- Everything you need to know to help you enjoy yourself and get the most out of your time away, from Accommodation through Baby-sitters, Car Hire, Food, Health, Money, Newspapers, Taxis, Telephones to Youth Hostels.

Cross-references:

Type in small capitals – CHURCHES – tells you that more information on an item is available within the topic on churches.

A-Z after an item tells you that more information is available within the gazetteer. Simply look under the appropriate name.

A name in bold – **Holy Cathedral** – also tells you that more information on an item is available in the gazetteer – again simply look up the name.

JORGE MANUEL GONÇALVE

CONTENTS

CONTENTS

INTRODUCTION

The Algarve, Portugal's southernmost province, has become one of the most popular destinations for British holiday-makers attracted by the sunshine and the superb sandy beaches which extend along its 160 km coastline. Bounded by the Atlantic Ocean to the south and west, the mountains of Caldeirão and Monchique to the north and by the river Guadiana to the east, the Algarve possesses a character distinct from the rest of Portugal. There is warm sunshine practically all the year round, the Gulf Stream and warm air currents from Africa ensure mild winters, and the summer heat is moderated by a welcoming breeze off the Atlantic. The increasing popularity of the region has stimulated intensive tourist development (some would say overdevelopment), with hotels, apartments and villas springing up indiscriminately along the coast. Between the major resorts, however, unspoilt beaches and picturesque coves can still be found, and inland, typical Algarvian villages with whitewashed houses and narrow streets retain much of their original charm.

The legacy of five centuries of Moorish rule (first established in the 8thC AD) is still prominent. The name Algarve is derived from the Arabic *Al Gharb*, meaning 'western land', and the legacy is also reflected in old fortifications, and in local architectural features such as the decorative chimneys and the use of hand-painted glazed tiles – *azulejos* – which adorn public buildings, churches and ordinary houses.

After the reconquest of the Algarve from the Moors, national rulers styled themselves 'Kings of Portugal and the Algarves', a title which reflects the separateness and isolation of the region.

This anonymity continued until the 15thC and the establishment of the School of Navigation at Sagres by Prince Henry the Navigator. Inspired by the researches of the prince and his team of renowned geographers, cartographers, nautical instrument-makers and master mariners, ships departed from Lagos on their voyages of discovery. By the time of Prince Henry's death in 1460, Portuguese explorers had discovered Madeira and the Azores, and charted the west coast of Africa as far as Sierra Leone.

The Age of Discovery in the late 15th/early 16thC marked the height of Portuguese wealth and power, but in the 18thC the Algarve was at the centre of the country's greatest misfortune. On 1 Nov. 1755 (All Saints'

BANCO
ALIANÇA
SEGURADORA
LIVRARIA
BERTRAND
tap
AIR PORTUGAL

Faro

Day) a catastrophic earthquake destroyed Lisbon in a matter of minutes; churches packed with worshippers collapsed and thousands of people died, their bodies washed out to sea by the accompanying tidal wave. The epicentre of the earthquake was just south of Lagos, and nearly all buildings in the towns and villages of the Algarve were completely destroyed.

The loss of so many historical buildings accounts for the lack of real distinction in local architecture, but this is more than compensated for by the superb scenery along the coastline. The character of the landscape and of the major towns varies from east to west. Most visitors fly to Faro, the provincial capital, and then immediately travel west to major resorts like Albufeira. For the sightseer, however, Faro contains much of interest. East of Faro are the attractive and relatively unspoilt towns of Olhão and Tavira set among rich agricultural land, and from Vila Real de Santo António you can visit Spain, only a few minutes' boat trip across the river Guadiana.

The major tourist developments are west of Faro. These include complexes such as Vale do Lobo and Vilamoura (the largest privately

planned tourist complex in Europe) which offer comprehensive sporting and entertainment facilities. Further west is Albufeira, the most popular resort on the coast, which manages to retain some of its Moorish character and charm amid the hotel and apartment complexes. Between Albufeira and Lagos are spectacular beaches stretching below ochre cliffs scarred by jagged rock formations and grottoes. Portimão is a large fishing port at the mouth of the river Arade, famous for its sardines and as a shopping centre. Opposite Portimão across the Arade estuary is Ferragudo, an unspoilt fishing village. West from Lagos, a bustling tourist centre celebrated for its connection with Henry the Navigator, the landscape becomes bleak and barren, blasted by the fierce winds off the Atlantic. Little evidence remains of Prince Henry's School of Navigation at Sagres. Much more impressive is Cape St. Vincent, the 'End of the World' – the most southwesterly point of mainland Europe. Various inland villages and towns are also worth exploring. In Loulé, a busy market town and handicrafts centre north of Faro, it is still possible to find genuine examples of Algarvian copper and brassware, cane furniture and wickerwork. Alte, in the hills northwest of Loulé, is the Algarve's most picturesque village. To the west, Silves is also a popular destination; from the battlements of its Moorish fortress there is a

wonderful view of the surrounding countryside. Northwest of Silves is the pretty spa village of Caldas de Monchique, famous for its pure spring water.

After a tiring day sunbathing or enjoying any one of the myriad activities available along the coast (such as windsurfing, golfing and horse riding), or after returning from an excursion inland to the mountains, indulge yourself with a wonderful fresh seafood dinner (grilled simply or incorporated into a delicious stew called *cataplana*) washed down with a bottle of *vinho verde*. Then round the evening off with one of the locally produced after-dinner drinks: Medronho, a strong wine distilled from red arbutus berries; chilled Amêndoa Amarga, made from bitter almonds; or Brandymel, a honey-flavoured brandy liqueur – the perfect end to a perfect day. If you still feel energetic you can prolong the evening at one of the many exciting nightspots offering varied entertainment, from soulful Fado music to the latest international club sounds. Whatever your holiday interests – whether sunshine, sport, nightlife, shopping for souvenirs, beautiful scenery or candlelit dinners – the Algarve is sure to please.

Callum Brines

COLLEGE

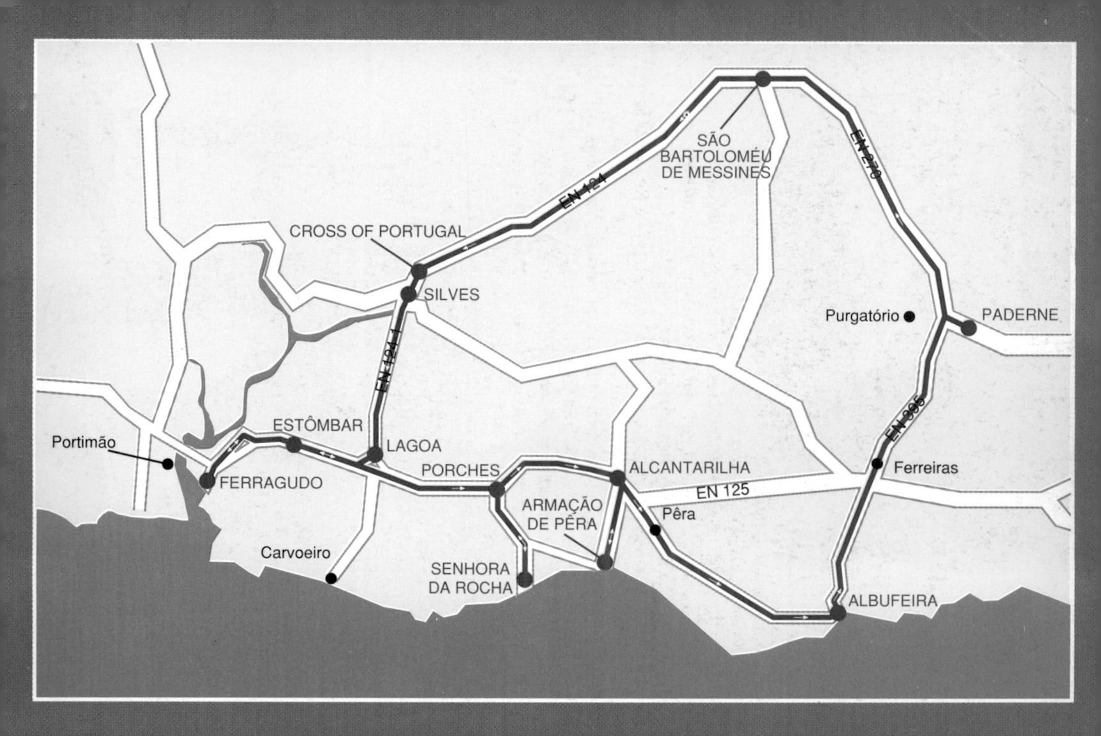
SÃO
BARTOLOMÉU
DE MESSINES
EN 270
EN 124
CROSS OF PORTUGAL
SILVES
Purgatório
PADERNE
EN 124-1
EN 395
Portimão
ESTÔMBAR
LAGOA
FERRAGUDO
PORCHES
ALCANTARILHA
Ferreiras
EN 125
ARMAÇÃO
DE PÊRA
Pêra
Carvoeiro
SENHORA
DA ROCHA
ALBUFEIRA

A one-day excursion exploring the western Barrocal (see **A-Z**), *Silves, and some of the most intriguing coves on the Algarve coastline.*

Take Route 595 from Albufeira towards Ferreiras then take the EN 395 towards São Bartoloméu de Messines.
13 km – Paderne. This village contains a 16thC Manueline (see **A-Z**) church with a magnificent *talha dourada* (see **A-Z**) altar. The ruined castle has an attractive gateway turret and the remains of a Gothic church. Drive back in the direction of Purgatório and then turn right at the junction of the EN 395 and EN 270.
25 km – São Bartoloméu de Messines. Visit the red sandstone Manueline church, decorated with cabled columns and *azulejos* (see **A-Z**). From São Bartoloméu head for Silves on the EN 124.
41 km – The Cross of Portugal. Just before Silves, this fine Renaissance statue is carved from white limestone.
42 km – Silves (see **A-Z**). The ancient capital of Muslim Algarve. Leave the town across the river Arade and take the EN 124-1 to Lagoa.
50 km – Lagoa. An important wine-producing centre. It has a Baroque parish church containing two polychrome statues of Nossa Senhora da Luz (16thC) and São Sebastião (18thC). The Igreja da Misericórdia is also worth a visit for its ornamental tiles. Head for Ferragudo on the EN 125 to Portimão.
53 km – Estômbar. An old Moorish town on the southern slope of a hill. It is the birthplace of the famous poet Ibn Ammar and has an attractive 16thC Manueline church. Turn left after Parchal onto the EN 530 to Ferragudo.
60 km – Ferragudo (see **BEACHES 2**). A picturesque fishing village with two beaches separated by an impressive fortress which, along with its twin, the Santa Catarina fortress on the opposite bank, dominates the estuary of the river Arade. Return along the same route to Parchal. Turn right on the EN 125 and follow the signs for Faro.
80 km – Porches. This is an important pottery-producing centre where you can visit some of the pottery workshops. On the right, just before you reach Porches, the EM 530-1 leads to the octagonal white chapel of Nossa Senhora da Rocha which perches above the ochre cliffs and tiny coves of this part of the coast (see **BEACHES 2**). In Porches itself,

Senhora da Rocha

don't miss the opportunity to visit O Leão, a gourmet restaurant which occupies a splendidly restored 17thC farmhouse.

85 km – Alcantarilha. A village typical of this coastal region, with its white houses decorated with pastel-coloured *azulejos,* and its lacework of chimney stacks and terraced roofs (*açoteias*). There is also a charming parish church with an attractive Manueline altar. From Alcantarilha it is 3 km to Armação de Pêra (see **A-Z**). Return to Alcantarilha, turn right to Pêra and follow the road back to Albufeira (95 km).

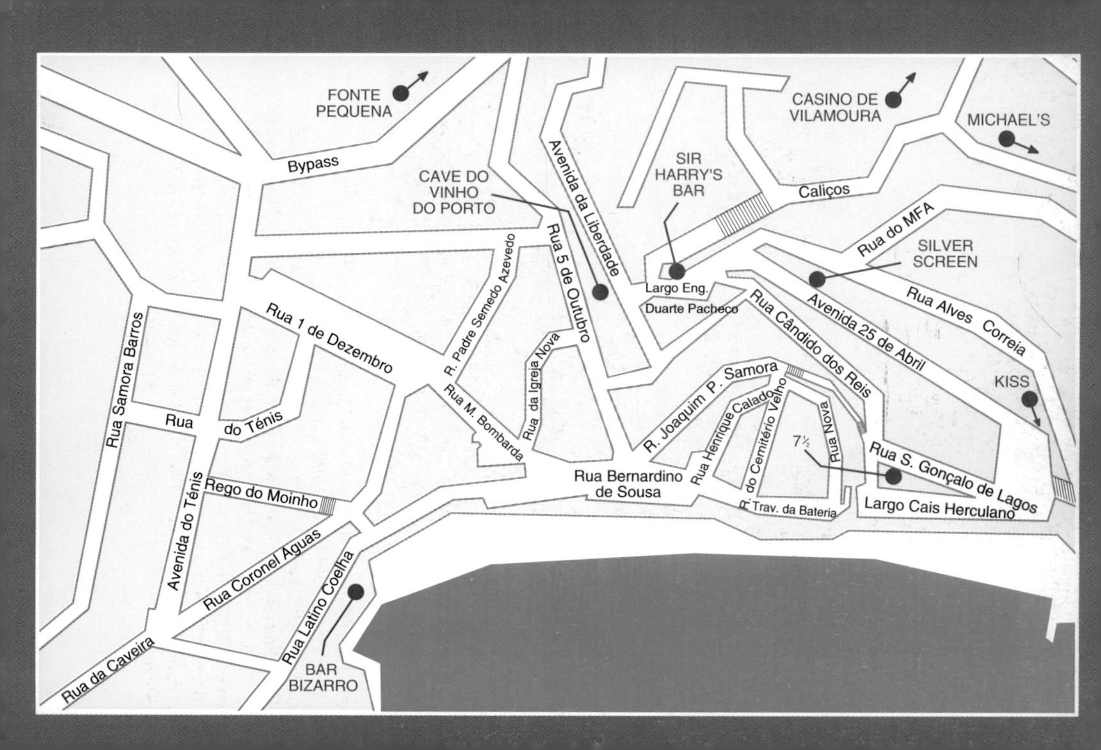
FONTE PEQUENA
CASINO DE VILAMOURA
MICHAEL'S
Bypass
CAVE DO VINHO DO PORTO
Avenida da Liberdade
SIR HARRY'S BAR
Caliços
Rua do MFA
SILVER SCREEN
Largo Eng. Duarte Pacheco
Rua Alves Correia
Avenida 25 de Abril
Rua Cândido dos Reis
KISS
R. Padre Semedo Azevedo
Rua 5 de Outubro
Rua 1 de Dezembro
Rua Samora Barros
Rua da Igreja Nova
Rua M. Bombarda
R. Joaquim P. Samora
Rua Henrique Calado
R. do Cemitério Velho
Rua Nova
7½
Rua S. Gonçalo de Lagos
Largo Cais Herculano
Trav. da Bateria
Rua Bernardino de Sousa
Rua do Ténis
Avenida do Ténis
Rego do Moinho
Rua Coronel Aguas
Rua Latino Coelha
Rua da Caveira
BAR BIZARRO

See **Opening Times**.

SIR HARRY'S BAR 37-38 Largo Eng. Duarte Pacheco.
A favourite with the older generation. Live music.

MICHAEL'S Montechoro, Albufeira. Beside the Hotel Montechoro.
Nightclub with cabaret for the whole family, featuring West End comedy/ musical productions.

BAR BIZARRO Esplanada Dr Frutuoso Silva. At west end of beach.
A quiet bar in a romantic setting – perfect at dusk.

SILVER SCREEN Avenida 25 de Abril.
■ Summer only.
The best club in town. Great lighting system and always lively.

KISS Areias de São João, 2 km outside Albufeira.
The longest-established disco in the area. Very busy in the summer.

CASINO DE VILAMOURA Marina de Vilamoura.
■ 1900-0300. ● 1000 Esc. for admission to gaming room.
Blackjack, roulette, slot machines, etc. as well as a restaurant and cabaret. Minimum bets are 500 Esc. (roulette) and 1000 Esc. (blackjack).

CAVE DO VINHO DO PORTO Avenida da Liberdade 23.
A haunt both for the connoisseurs of vintage port and for those who have never tried it before. Live music.

7 1/2 Largo Cais Herculano 7.
This is the best disco in the centre of town. It is extremely popular and always crowded in summer.

FONTE PEQUENA Alte, 24 km north of Albufeira.
Regular excursions visit this folklore and barbecue evening. There are whirling dancers and local musicians, and you can eat and drink as much as you like.

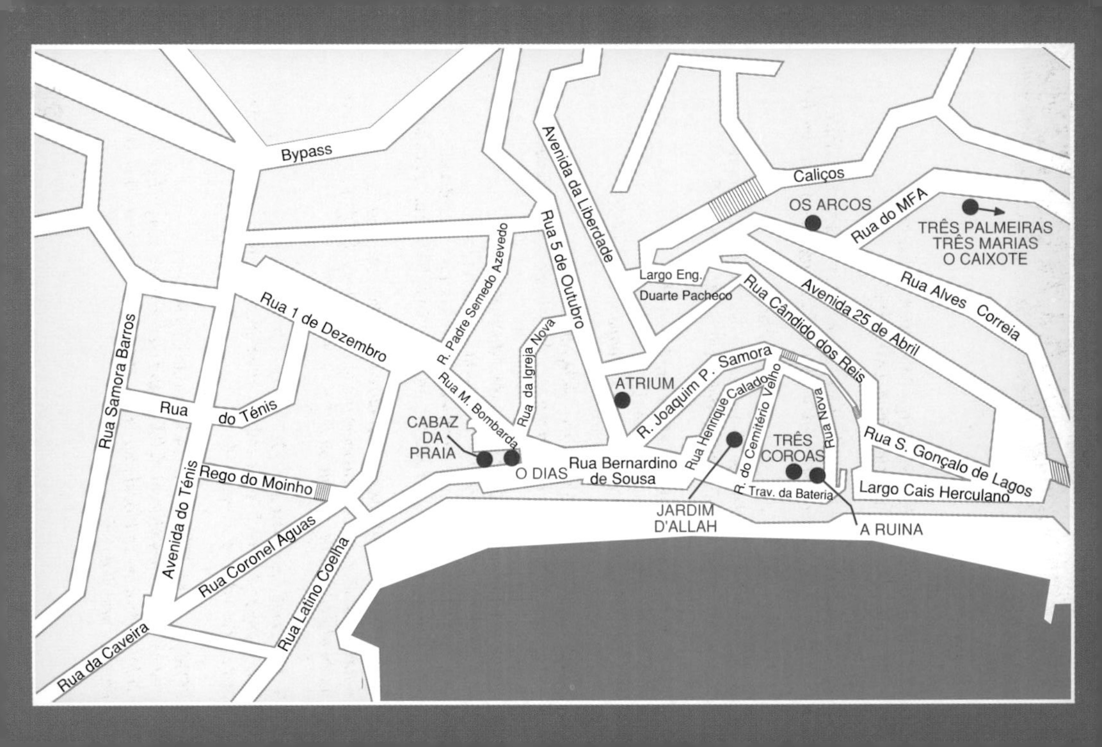
Bypass
Caliços
OS ARCOS
Rua do MFA
TRÊS PALMEIRAS
TRÊS MARIAS
O CAIXOTE
Avenida da Liberdade
Rua 5 de Outubro
Largo Eng.
Duarte Pacheco
Rua Alves Correia
Avenida 25 de Abril
Rua Cândido dos Reis
Rua 1 de Dezembro
R. Padre Semedo Azevedo
Rua da Igreja Nova
ATRIUM
R. Joaquim P. Samora
Rua Henrique Calado
R. do Cemitério Velho
Rua Nova
TRÊS COROAS
Rua S. Gonçalo de Lagos
Largo Cais Herculano
Trav. da Bateria
A RUINA
JARDIM D'ALLAH
Rua Bernardino de Sousa
O DIAS
Rua M. Bombarda
CABAZ DA PRAIA
Rua Samora Barros
Rua do Ténis
Avenida do Ténis
Rego do Moinho
Rua Coronel Aguas
Rua Latino Coelha
Rua da Caveira

See **Opening Times**.

A RUINA Praia dos Pescadores. ● Expensive.
Overlooking the sea. The most atmospheric restaurant in town.

JARDIM D'ALLAH Beco José Bernardino de Souza. ● Expensive.
Excellent Arab cuisine served in a Moorish setting.

CABAZ DA PRAIA Praça Miguel Bombarda.
■ Closed Thu. ● Expensive.
Enjoy excellent French cuisine on a beautiful cliff-side terrace.

ATRIUM Rua 5 de Outubro 20. ● Moderate-Expensive.
Refined international and local cuisine with excellent service.

O DIAS Praça Miguel Bombarda. ● Moderate.
The best grilled food in Albufeira. Has a terrace overlooking the sea.

TRÊS COROAS Rua Correio Valho 8. ● Moderate.
The most attractive terrace in town. Popular with British tourists.

OS ARCOS Rua Alves Correira 25. ● Moderate.
A fine Portuguese restaurant which specializes in seafood.

TRÊS PALMEIRAS Areias de São João, Albufeira.
■ Closed Sun. ● Moderate.
Barbecue grills and seafood which are popular with locals and tourists alike. Recommended.

TRÊS MARIAS Olhos de Água, Albufeira. Between Olhos de Água and the Hotel Balaia. ● Moderate.
Large choice of barbecued food, grilled fish, seafood. Friendly service.

O CAIXOTE Praia de Olhos de Água, Albufeira. Right on the beach.
● Inexpensive.
Perfect for a lunch in the shade.

MEIA PRAIA
Odiáxere
MOURANITOS
BURGAU
PRAIA DA LUZ
Lagos
DONA ANA-CAMILO
Budens
CASTELEJO
Vila do Bispo
Figueira
SALEMA
BELICHE
BALEEIRA
Cabo de São Vincente
Sagres

CASTELEJO–MOURANITOS Vila do Bispo.
Vast empty beaches 4-10 km west of Vila do Bispo. Good for swimming, sunbathing and windsurfing. See **LAGOS-EXCURSION 2**.

BELICHE
2 km west of Sagres on the EN 268.
Lying below a small fort, this is the closest beach to the 'World's End'.

BALEEIRA Sagres.
A very small beach at the east end of the town, popular for scuba diving and deep-sea fishing.

SALEMA
On the EM 537 from Budens.
A lovely beach situated below a fishing village, with several restaurants and facilities for horse riding and water sports. See **LAGOS-EXCURSION 2**.

BURGAU
15 km west of Lagos.
A small beach below an 18thC fortress. Facilities include restaurants, a horse-riding centre and water sports. See **LAGOS-EXCURSION 2**.

PRAIA DA LUZ
8 km west of Lagos on the EM 534.
A large, beautiful beach offering a wide range of activities, from tennis to scuba diving. See **LAGOS-EXCURSION 2, NIGHTLIFE**.

DONA ANA–CAMILO Lagos.
Extending from Ponta da Piedade to Lagos, this garland of sandy coves nestled below cliffs is laced with arches and caves. There are hotels and restaurants nearby.

MEIA PRAIA
2 km east of Lagos.
Lagos's largest beach, with hotels, restaurants, tennis courts, a golf course and water-sports facilities.

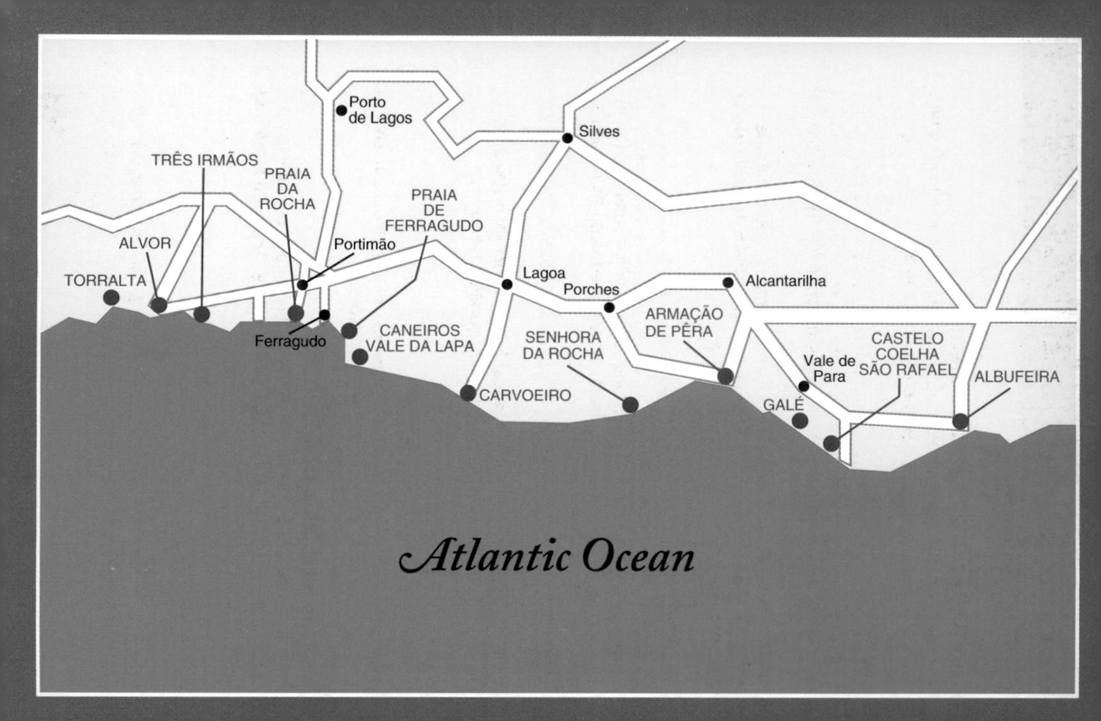
Porto de Lagos
Silves
TRÊS IRMÃOS
PRAIA DA ROCHA
PRAIA DE FERRAGUDO
ALVOR
Portimão
TORRALTA
Lagoa
Porches
Alcantarilha
ARMAÇÃO DE PÊRA
Ferragudo
CANEIROS
VALE DA LAPA
SENHORA DA ROCHA
CASTELO
COELHA
SÃO RAFAEL
Vale de Para
ALBUFEIRA
GALÉ
CARVOEIRO
Atlantic Ocean

TORRALTA–ALVOR–TRÊS IRMÃOS
Alvor, 5 km west of Portimão on the EM 5311.
A long, flat stretch with hotels and rock formations at the eastern end.

PRAIA DA ROCHA 4 km south of Portimão on the EN 124.
The Algarve's most famous beach, with fantastic rock formations and a range of water sports. See PORTIMÃO-ATTRACTIONS.

PRAIA DE FERRAGUDO 3 km from Portimão across the Arade.
Two lovely beaches overlooked by twin forts. There are restaurants and a windsurfing school. See ALBUFEIRA-EXCURSION.

CANEIROS–VALE DA LAPA 2 km south of Ferragudo.
Two typically quiet and attractive beaches, the second of which is accessible only on foot.

CARVOEIRO 5 km from Lagoa on the EN 124-1.
A small, pretty beach lying beneath a picturesque fishing village.

SENHORA DA ROCHA
5 km from Porches and 4 km from Armação de Pêra.
Three small beaches. From the scuba-diving centre you can explore the area's underwater world. See ALBUFEIRA-EXCURSION.

ARMAÇÃO DE PÊRA 18 km west of Albufeira.
One of the Algarve's longest and most popular beaches. There are large resort facilities at the eastern end and quiet coves to the west. See ALBUFEIRA-EXCURSION, A-Z.

GALÉ–CASTELO–COELHA–SÃO RAFAEL
6 km west of Albufeira, via Vale da Para.
Lovely, quiet, sandy coves easily accessible from Albufeira.

ALBUFEIRA
Two beaches on either side of the Old Town. The main one, Praia do Poente, can be reached through a tunnel under the Hotel Sol e Mar.

Guia
Albufeira
OURA BALAIA
MARIA LUISA
OLHOS DE ÁGUA
Boliqueime
FALÉSIA
VILAMOURA
Loulé
QUARTEIRA
Almansil
VALE DO LOBO
GARRÃO ANÇÃO
Quinta do Lago
PRAIA DE FARO
São Brás de Alportel
Faro

OURA–BALAIA
4 km east of Albufeira via Areias de São João.
Two reasonably sized yet crowded beaches with tennis courts, sailing, windsurfing and water-skiing.

MARIA LUISA
5 km east of Albufeira, just before Olhos de Água.
A pretty, little beach frequented by naturists.

OLHOS DE ÁGUA
6 km east of Albufeira.
Fine, shell-shaped beach. Good facilities and superb La Cigale restaurant.

FALÉSIA
East of Olhos de Água.
A long, uninterrupted series of beaches running below cliffs and sand dunes all the way to Vilamoura.

VILAMOURA
Long, sandy beach. Many hotels and restaurants. Sports facilities, marina.

QUARTEIRA
A large, busy beach lined with apartment buildings and hotels. Tennis and windsurfing facilities.

VALE DO LOBO
6 km south of Almansil.
An enormous tourist complex with a full range of sports facilities.

GARRÃO–ANÇÃO
3 km from Quinta do Lago.
A vast expanse of sand beside the Ria Formosa nature reserve.

PRAIA DE FARO
7 km from Faro on the airport road.
A long, narrow, popular family beach with restaurants, hotels and bars.

ILHA
DE TAVIRA
Tavira
Pedras
de Rainha
CABANAS
Vila Nova
de Cacela
CACELA
MANTA
ROTA
PRAIA
VERDE
MONTE
GORDO
Vila Real
de Santo
António
Pedras de El-Rei
Santa Luzia
BARRIL
Luz
FUZETA
Fuzeta
FAROL
HANGARES
CULATRA
Olhão

FAROL–HANGARES–CULATRA
20 min by boat from Olhão, on Ilha do Farol and Ilha da Culatra.
Vast, quiet barrier-island beaches ideal for getting away from it all.

FUZETA
10 km east of Olhão.
A family beach beside a fishing village, with a lagoon for fishing, sailing and windsurfing. See FARO-EXCURSION 2.

BARRIL
Pedras del Rey, Santa Luzia, 6 km west of Tavira.
An extensive beach beside a holiday centre, with restaurants and horse riding, and water-skiing and windsurfing facilities.

ILHA DE TAVIRA
Santa Luzia, 3 km east of Tavira. Boat from Tavira.
The beach lies in front of the charming harbour of Santa Luzia.

CABANAS Pedras de Rainha, Cabanas, 8 km east of Tavira.
Lovely beach at the Pedras de Rainha tourist village. Open to day visitors. See FARO-EXCURSION 2.

CACELA
Vila Nova de Cacela, 12 km east of Tavira.
A picturesque beach lying at the foot of an ancient Arab village. There are facilities for fishing and windsurfing. See FARO-EXCURSION 2.

MANTA ROTA–PRAIA VERDE
11 km west of Vila Real de Santo António.
Broad, long beaches backed by dunes and some pine woods. Calm waters make them suitable for families. See FARO-EXCURSION 2.

MONTE GORDO Vila Real de Santo António, 4 km west of Vila Real.
A very popular resort with a large beach backed by pine woods. There are water-sports facilities, restaurants, hotels and a casino. See FARO-EXCURSION 2.

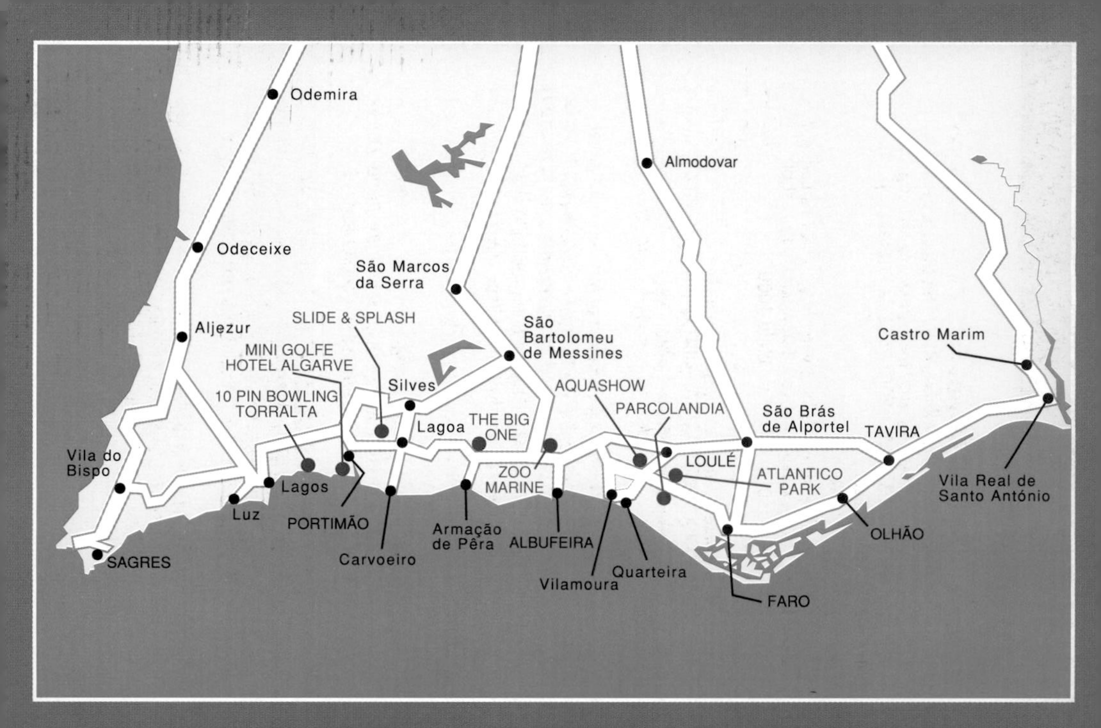
Odemira
Odeceixe
Aljezur
Vila do Bispo
SAGRES
Luz
Lagos
PORTIMÃO
10 PIN BOWLING TORRALTA
MINI GOLFE HOTEL ALGARVE
SLIDE & SPLASH
São Marcos da Serra
Silves
Lagoa
Carvoeiro
THE BIG ONE
Armação de Pêra
São Bartolomeu de Messines
ZOO MARINE
ALBUFEIRA
AQUASHOW
Almodovar
PARCOLANDIA
Vilamoura
Quarteira
LOULÉ
ATLANTICO PARK
São Brás de Alportel
FARO
OLHÃO
TAVIRA
Castro Marim
Vila Real de Santo António

10 PIN BOWLING TORRALTA Torre C, Praia de Torralta, Alvor, 6 km west of Portimão. ■ 1400-0200. ● 350 Esc.

MINI GOLFE HOTEL ALGARVE Praia da Rocha, Portimão.
■ 1000-2100. ● 500 Esc.
A popular 18-hole course.

SLIDE & SPLASH On the EN 125, Estombar, 7 km east of Portimão. ■ 1000-1900. ● 1500 Esc., child 1000 Esc.
The latest thing in thrilling water slides.

THE BIG ONE On the EN 125, Alcantarilha, 10 km west of Albufeira. ■ 1000-1900 summer. ● 1500 Esc., child 1000 Esc.
Big-wave swimming pools, slides and rapids, plus mini golf.

ZOO MARINE On the EN 125, Guia, 6 km northwest of Albufeira.
■ 1000-2200 summer, 1000-1800 winter. ● 1500 Esc., child 1000 Esc.
Florida-style amusement park with performing dolphins, sea lions and an elephant seal. Also parrot shows, a 180° cinema, children's fairground rides and swimming pools.

AQUASHOW On the EN 396, near Quatro Estradas, 5 km north of Quarteira. ■ 1000-1800.
An aqua-amusement park with water slides, inner-tube rides and a wave pool, plus a thrill ride simulator and Grand Prix mini-Formula 1 racing cars for adults and children.

ATLANTICO PARK On the EN 125, near Quatro Estradas, 5 km north of Quarteira. ■ 1000-1800 summer. ● 1500 Esc., child 1000 Esc.
Water slides, rapid rides, a bouncy castle, go-karts and a daily high-diving spectacular.

PARCOLANDIA On the EN 125, Almansil.
■ Daily shows at 1100 & 1600. ● 1500 Esc., child 1000 Esc.
Wild West theme park with fairground rides, and shows where dancers and singers revive the romance of the classic Western.

Olhos de Água

AL-7 L
NOVA-PRAIA-DA-OURA

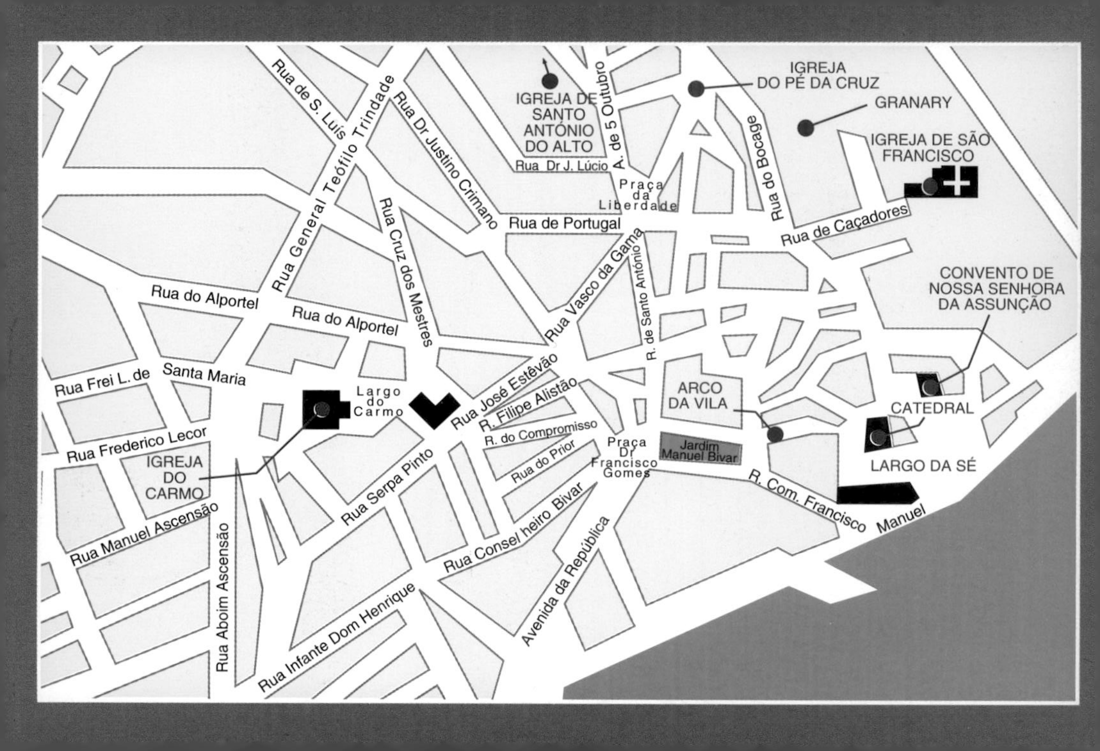
IGREJA DO PÉ DA CRUZ
GRANARY
IGREJA DE SÃO FRANCISCO
IGREJA DE SANTO ANTÓNIO DO ALTO
Rua de S. Luís
Rua General Teófilo Trindade
Rua Dr Justino Crimano
Rua Dr J. Lúcio
A. de 5 Outubro
Praça da Liberdade
Rua do Bocage
Rua de Caçadores
Rua de Portugal
CONVENTO DE NOSSA SENHORA DA ASSUNÇÃO
Rua do Alportel
Rua do Alportel
Rua Cruz dos Mestres
Rua Vasco da Gama
R. de Santo António
ARCO DA VILA
CATEDRAL
Rua Frei L. de Santa Maria
Largo do Carmo
Rua José Estêvão
R. Filipe Alistão
R. do Compromisso
Rua do Prior
Praça Dr Francisco Gomes
Jardim Manuel Bivar
LARGO DA SÉ
Rua Frederico Lecor
IGREJA DO CARMO
Rua Serpa Pinto
R. Com. Francisco Manuel
Rua Manuel Ascensão
Rua Consel heiro Bivar
Rua Aboim Ascensão
Avenida da República
Rua Infante Dom Henrique

CATEDRAL (SÉ) Largo da Sé, Old Town.
■ 0800-1200, 1430-1700.
A notable Renaissance church, the interior walls of which are ornamented with azulejos *(see* **A-Z***). Organ recitals are given during the summer.*

CONVENTO DE NOSSA SENHORA DA ASSUNÇÃO
Largo Dom Afonso III, Old Town.
Contains a magnificent Renaissance cloister and houses the Museu Arqueológico Infante Dom Henrique (see **FARO-MUSEUMS***).*

ARCO DA VILA At the eastern end of the Jardim Manuel Bivar, next to the tourist office.
The main gate of the Old Town, designed in a simple but beautiful 18thC Italian style. Look out for the resident storks.

IGREJA DE SÃO FRANCISCO Largo de São Francisco. In a square behind the Old Town. ■ Open for services only.
A church whose 18thC azulejos *(tiles) depict the life of São Francisco. There is also valuable gilded and carved woodwork in the chancel.*

GRANARY Off Rua do Bocage.
Hexagonal-shaped granary with bas-reliefs of mythological figures.

LARGO DA SÉ Old Town.
The large cathedral square, filled with orange trees.

IGREJA DO CARMO Largo do Carmo.
■ 1000-1200, 1600-1700.
Baroque church with a Capela dos Ossos, which has bone-covered walls.

IGREJA DO PÉ DA CRUZ Largo do Pé da Cruz.
Contains 17thC frescoes depicting scenes from the Pentecost.

IGREJA DE SANTO ANTÓNIO DO ALTO Rua de Berlim.
Simple Baroque deconsecrated church with breathtaking views of Faro. Near is a small museum devoted to Santo António. See **FARO-MUSEUMS**.

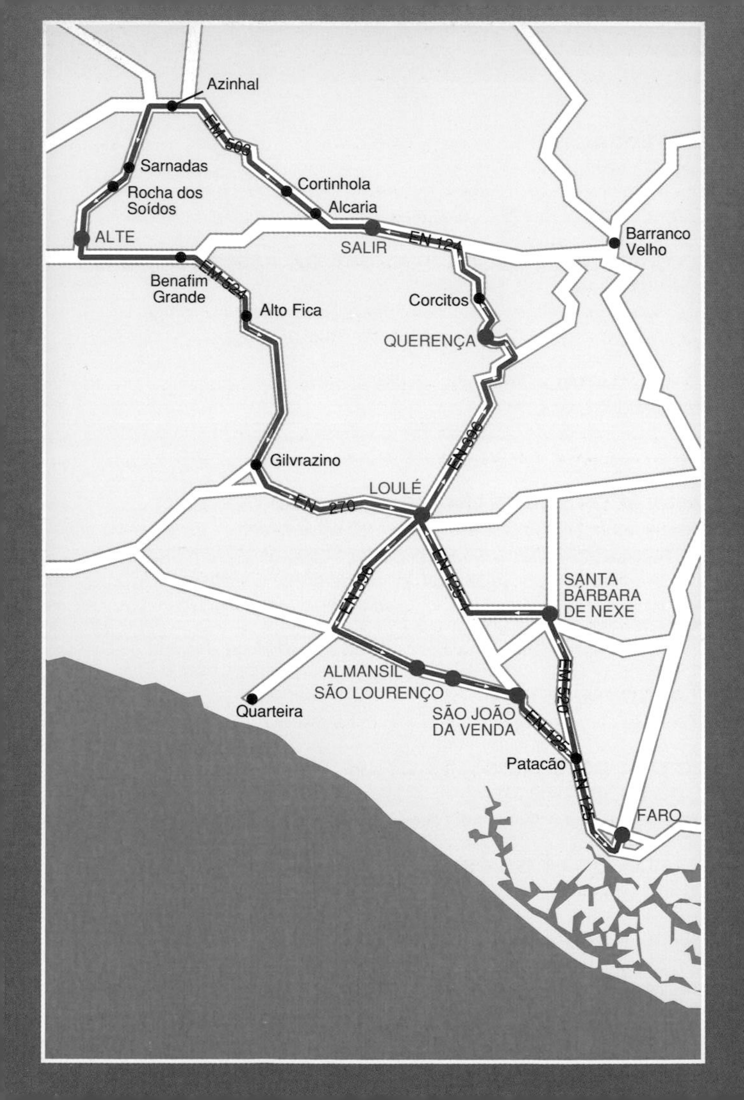

Azinhal
EM 503
Sarnadas
Rocha dos Soídos
Cortinhola
Alcaria
ALTE
SALIR
EN 124
Barranco Velho
Benafim Grande
EM 524
Alto Fica
Corcitos
QUERENÇA
EN 396
Gilvrazino
LOULÉ
EN 270
EN 396
EN 125-4
SANTA BÁRBARA DE NEXE
ALMANSIL
SÃO LOURENÇO
SÃO JOÃO DA VENDA
EM 520
EN 125
Quarteira
Patacão
EN 125
FARO

Excursion 1

A one-day excursion to Loulé, visiting some of the villages characteristic of the Barrocal (see **A-Z***).*

Leave Faro on the EN 125 towards Portimão. After 6 km, at Patacão, turn right onto the EM 520.

12 km – Santa Bárbara de Nexe (see **A-Z**). Follow the signs back to the EN 125-4 and turn right towards Loulé.

20 km – Loulé (see **A-Z**). An important market town. Leave Loulé, following the signs for Lisbon, on the EN 396. After 10 km turn left and left again onto the EM 524 to Querença and Salir.

31 km – Querença. A picturesque village with an interesting 16thC church. Follow the signs for Tôr, then after 1 km turn right onto the EN 150 for Corcitos.

33 km – Fonte de Benemola and the caves of Salustreira and Igrejinha dos Mouros. Follow the road for Corcitos until you reach the EN 124, then turn left to Salir and Alte.

41 km – Salir. An old village overlooked by the remains of an Arab fortress. It has a beautiful church housing a richly illuminated papal bull dating from 1550. After 1 km turn right to Alcaria on the EM 503 towards the villages of Cortinhola, Soalheira and Azinhal. From Azinhal, follow the road down to Alte through Sarnadas and Rocha dos Soídos.

60 km – Alte (see **A-Z**). One of the prettiest villages in the Algarve. Drive back onto the EN 124 towards Barranco. After 5 km, at Benafim Grande, turn right onto the EM 524 to Alto Fica and follow the road to the junction with the EN 270 after Gilvrazino and then turn left towards Loulé. In Loulé, turn right and take the EN 396 towards Quarteira. After 5 km, beyond Loulé station, turn left on the EN 125.

95 km – Almansil. A crossroads market town famous for its ceramics.

98 km – São Lourenço. There is a beautiful Romanesque chapel here, the interior of which is completely covered with 18thC *azulejos* (see **A-Z**) depicting São Lourenço's life.

100 km – São João da Venda. The parish church here exhibits various elements of Manueline (see **A-Z**) architecture. Continue on the EN 125 back to Faro (108 km).

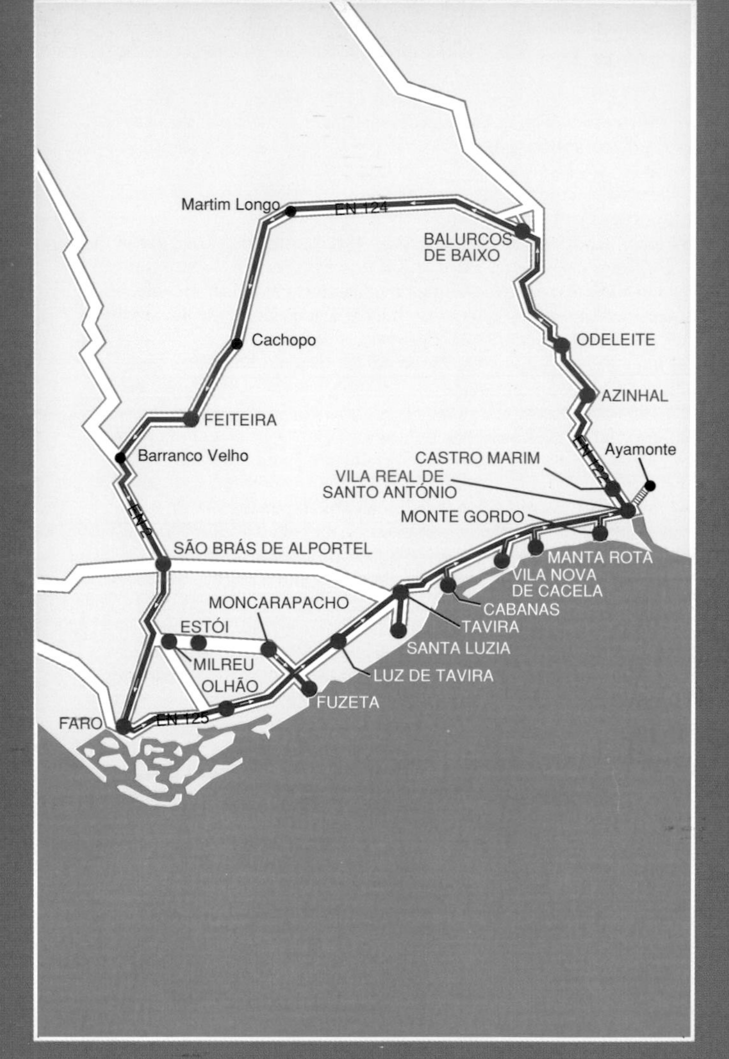

Martim Longo
EN 124
BALURCOS
DE BAIXO
Cachopo
ODELEITE
AZINHAL
FEITEIRA
Barranco Velho
EN 122
Ayamonte
CASTRO MARIM
VILA REAL DE
SANTO ANTÓNIO
MONTE GORDO
EN 2
SÃO BRÁS DE ALPORTEL
MANTA ROTA
VILA NOVA
DE CACELA
CABANAS
MONCARAPACHO
TAVIRA
ESTÓI
SANTA LUZIA
MILREU
OLHÃO
LUZ DE TAVIRA
FUZETA
FARO
EN 125

Excursion 2

A one-day excursion exploring the shores of the Sotavento, the left bank of the Guadiana river, the Serra do Caldeirão and the peaceful villages of the Barrocal (see **A-Z***).*

Leave Faro on the EN 125 towards Tavira.
8 km – Olhão (see **A-Z**). An important fishing village with a pleasant 18thC harbour. After 10 km a road on the right leads to Fuzeta (see **BEACHES 4**), a charming little fishing village lying at the far end of the lagoon. On the left is the road to Moncarapacho (see **A-Z**). Return to the main road after these detours.
24 km – Luz de Tavira. The Renaissance parish church here has attractive Manueline (see **A-Z**) gates.
31 km – Tavira (see **A-Z**). Nearby are Santa Luzia and Cabanas (see **BEACHES 4**). A further 12 km along on the right is the road to Vila Nova de Cacela (see **BEACHES 4**), which contains the ruins of a medieval fortress and a beautiful church portal. Along the next 5 km are the beaches of Manta Rota and Monte Gordo (see **BEACHES 4**).
53 km – Vila Real de Santo António (see **A-Z**). From Vila Real you can take a trip on the ferry across to Ayamonte in Spain (remember to bring your passport, just in case anyone at the border wishes to see it) or take the EN 122, just before Vila Real, which leads through the Sapal de Castro Marim nature reserve, a mosaic of salt marshes.
56 km – Castro Marim (see **A-Z**). Turn right, following signs for Lisbon.
65 km – Azinhal. A pleasant village overlooking the river Guadiana.
73 km – Odeleite. A curious village nestled in the bottom of a gully.
90 km – Balurcos de Baixo. In the foothills of the Serra do Caldeirão. Turn left on the EN 124 which leads via Martim Longo (23 km) and Cachopo to Barranco Velho (40 km) through the highlands of the Algarve, a wild moorland landscape. There are magnificent views over the valley of the Odeleite river, especially from the village of Feiteira, 10 km south of Cachopo on the EN 124. At Barranco the EN 124 joins the EN 2 for Faro.
167 km – São Brás de Alportel (see **A-Z**).
176 km – Estói & Milreu (see **A-Z**). These ruins lie 1 km off the EN 2 on the road to Olhão, 7 km south of São Brás de Alportel. Return to the EN 2 and continue into Faro (185 km).

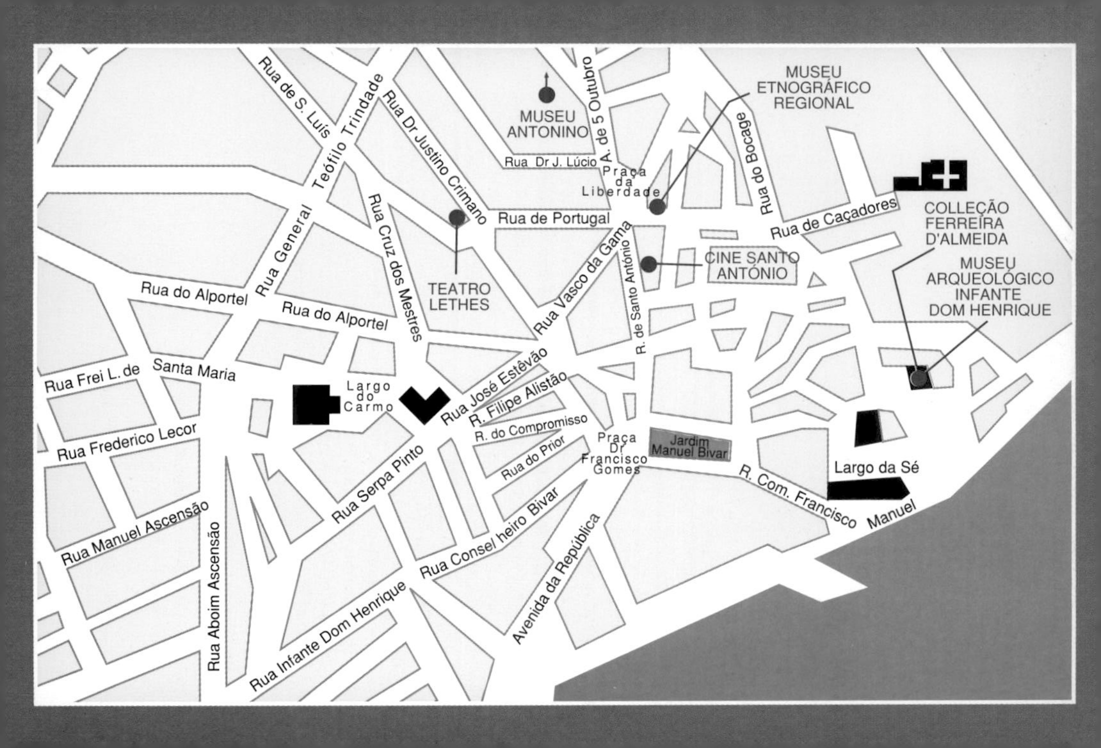

MUSEU ANTONINO
MUSEU ETNOGRÁFICO REGIONAL
COLLEÇÃO FERREIRA D'ALMEIDA
MUSEU ARQUEOLÓGICO INFANTE DOM HENRIQUE
Rua de S. Luís
Teófilo Trindade
Rua General
Rua Dr Justino Crimano
A. de 5 Outubro
Rua Dr J. Lúcio
Praça da Liberdade
Rua do Bocage
Rua de Caçadores
Rua de Portugal
TEATRO LETHES
Rua Cruz dos Mestres
Rua Vasco da Gama
R. de Santo António
CINE SANTO ANTÓNIO
Rua do Alportel
Rua do Alportel
Rua Frei L. de Santa Maria
Largo do Carmo
Rua José Estêvão
R. Filipe Alistão
R. do Compromisso
Rua do Prior
Praça Dr Francisco Gomes
Jardim Manuel Bivar
Largo da Sé
R. Com. Francisco Manuel
Rua Frederico Lecor
Rua Serpa Pinto
Rua Manuel Ascensão
Rua Aboim Ascensão
Rua Consel heiro Bivar
Avenida da República
Rua Infante Dom Henrique

MUSEU ARQUEOLÓGICO INFANTE DOM HENRIQUE

Convento de Nossa Senhora da Assunção, Largo Dom Afonso III.
0900-1200, 1400-1700 Mon.-Fri. Inexpensive.
Houses important examples of Portuguese art, and prehistoric and Roman finds, including a large floor mosaic. *See* FARO-ATTRACTIONS.

COLLEÇÂO FERREIRA D'ALMEIDA

Inside the Museu Arqueológico Infante D. Henrique (see above).
0900-1200, 1400-1700 Mon.-Fri. Inexpensive.
An original collection of paintings, sculpture, Gauguin drawings and furniture.

MUSEU ETNOGRÁFICO REGIONAL

Praça da Liberdade.
0930-1230, 1400-1730 Mon.-Fri. Inexpensive.
An interesting collection of local crafts, ceramics, embroidery, costumes, photographs, life-size tableaux and other exhibits evoking traditional life.

MUSEU ANTONINO

Igreja Santo António do Alto, Rua de Berlim. In the church annex.
0930-1200, 1430-1730. Inexpensive.
Exhibits items relating to the life and times of Santo António. *See* FARO-ATTRACTIONS.

TEATRO LETHES

Rua Dr Justino Crimano. In the former Jesuit college.
The cultural centre of the town, and the venue for visiting ballet companies and orchestras. The building is in the Italianate style, with an interesting ceiling and stage curtain.

CINE SANTO ANTÓNIO

Rua Santo António 29.
Performances at 1600 & 2130.
Faro's only cinema is in the Galerias Santo António shopping centre. Undubbed major English-language films are regularly shown.

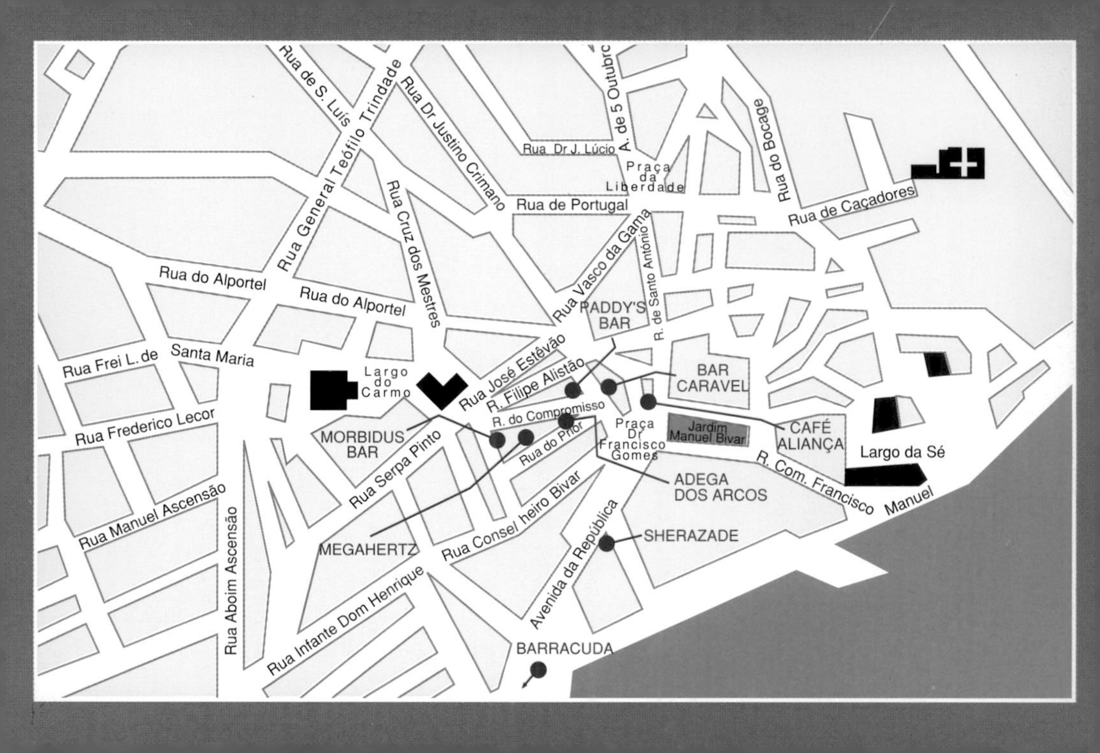

Rua de S. Luís
Rua General Teófilo Trindade
Rua Dr Justino Crimano
A. de 5 Outubro
Rua Dr J. Lúcio
Praça da Liberdade
Rua do Bocage
Rua de Portugal
Rua de Caçadores
Rua Cruz dos Mestres
Rua Vasco da Gama
R. de Santo António
Rua do Alportel
Rua do Alportel
PADDY'S BAR
BAR CARAVEL
Rua Frei L. de Santa Maria
Largo do Carmo
Rua José Estêvão
R. Filipe Alistão
R. do Compromisso
Praça Dr Francisco Gomes
Jardim Manuel Bivar
CAFÉ ALIANÇA
Largo da Sé
Rua Frederico Lecor
MORBIDUS BAR
Rua do Prior
Rua Serpa Pinto
ADEGA DOS ARCOS
R. Com. Francisco Manuel
Rua Manuel Ascensão
Rua Conselheiro Bivar
Rua Aboim Ascensão
MEGAHERTZ
Avenida da República
SHERAZADE
Rua Infante Dom Henrique
BARRACUDA

Nightlife

See **Opening Times**.

SHERAZADE
Hotel Eva, beside the marina.
Bar and disco popular with the older generation. Really for hotel guests only, although all tourists are welcome.

MEGAHERTZ
Rua do Prior 38.
The best disco in town, popular with locals and tourists.

BARRACUDA
Praia de Faro.
The only disco club on the beach.

ADEGA DOS ARCOS
Rua do Prior 15. On the corner of Rua do Prior and Travessa dos Arcos.
Spacious restaurant and bar with regular Fado (see **A-Z***) evenings.*

BAR CARAVEL
Rua do Compromisso.
A small and attractively decorated bar which is popular with both locals and tourists.

PADDY'S BAR
Rua do Compromisso.
The décor and seating is more austere here than in Bar Caravel (see above) but this bar is still full of character.

MORBIDUS BAR
Travessa de São Pedro 7a.
A small and intimate bar with delicate azulejo *(see* **A-Z***) décor.*

CAFÉ ALIANÇA
Rua Dr Francisco Gomes.
The meeting point for young and old, tourists and locals alike.

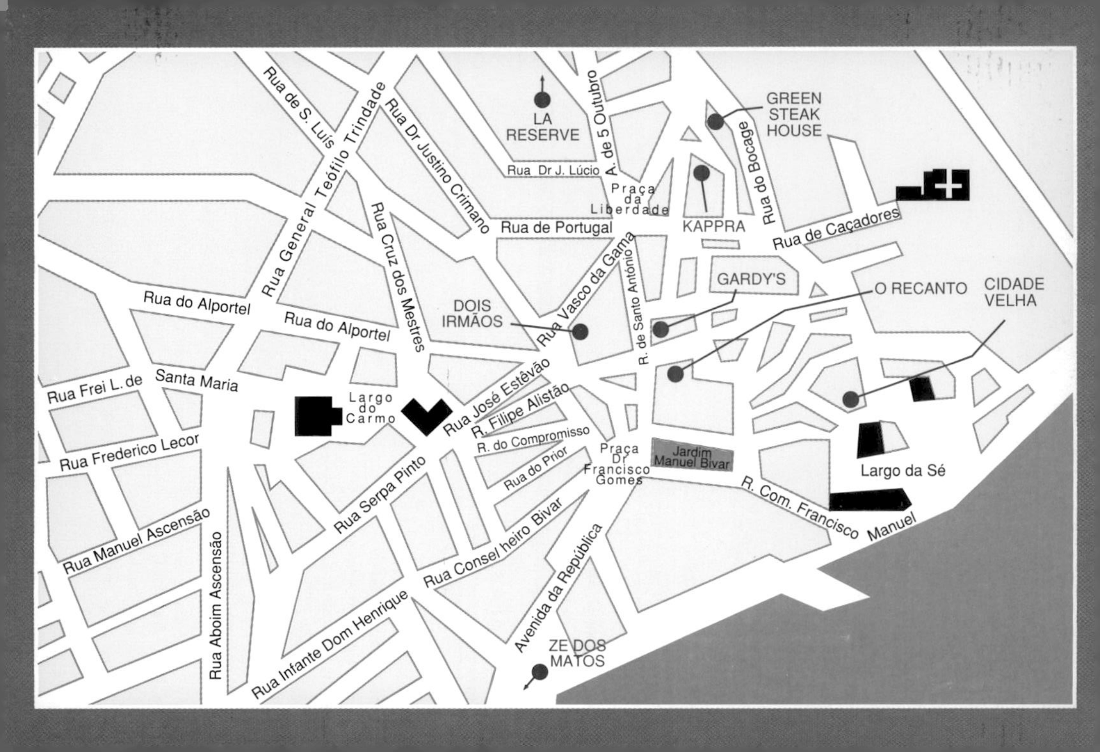

LA RESERVE
GREEN STEAK HOUSE
KAPPRA
GARDY'S
O RECANTO
CIDADE VELHA
DOIS IRMÃOS
ZE DOS MATOS
Rua de S. Luís
Rua General Teófilo Trindade
Rua Dr Justino Crimano
Rua Dr J. Lúcio
A. de 5 Outubro
Praça da Liberdade
Rua de Portugal
Rua do Bocage
Rua de Caçadores
Rua Cruz dos Mestres
Rua do Alportel
Rua do Alportel
Rua Vasco da Gama
R. de Santo António
Rua Frei L. de Santa Maria
Largo do Carmo
Rua José Estêvão
R. Filipe Alistão
R. do Compromisso
Rua do Prior
Praça Dr Francisco Gomes
Jardim Manuel Bivar
Largo da Sé
R. Com. Francisco Manuel
Rua Frederico Lecor
Rua Serpa Pinto
Rua Manuel Ascensão
Rua Aboim Ascensão
Rua Consel heiro Bivar
Avenida da República
Rua Infante Dom Henrique

See **Opening Times**.

CIDADE VELHA Rua Domingos Guieiro, Largo da Sé.
Closed Sun. Expensive.
The best food in Faro served in exclusive and elegant surroundings.

LA RESERVE
Between Esteval and Santa Bárbara de Nexe, 8 km from Faro.
Closed Tue. Expensive.
Superb French and Portuguese cuisine in a magnificent garden setting.

GREEN STEAK HOUSE Rua Pé da Cruz.
Moderate-Expensive.
Seafood and Portuguese specialities. Superb service.

ZE DOS MATOS Praia de Faro.
Moderate.
Excellent fish and shellfish in a family-run establishment.

DOIS IRMÃOS Rua Terreiro do Bispo 20.
Moderate.
Excellent local food in one of the oldest restaurants in the Algarve.

O RECANTO Rua 1 Dezembro 28.
Closed Sun. Moderate.
British-run establishment offering imaginative European cuisine.

KAPPRA Rua Brites de Almeida 45.
Moderate.
Restaurant serving inventive local dishes.

GARDY'S
Rua de Santo António 16. In the central pedestrian area.
Inexpensive-Moderate.
Has excellent sandwiches and sweets.

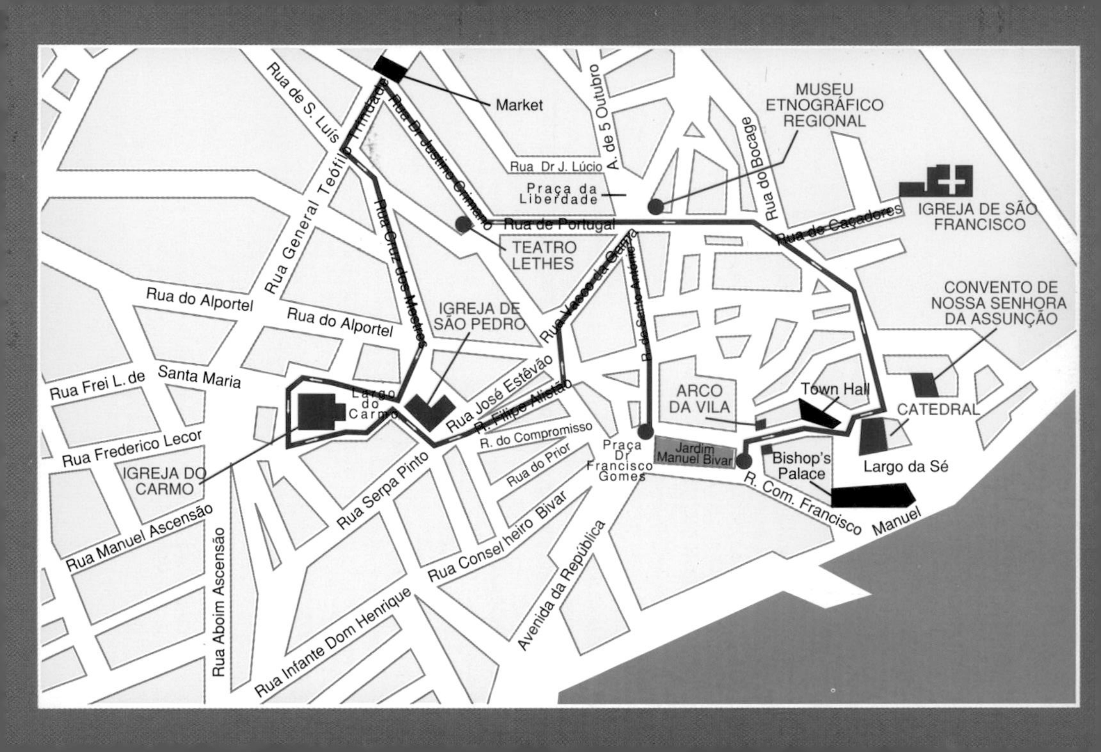
Market
MUSEU ETNOGRÁFICO REGIONAL
Rua de S. Luís
Rua General Teófilo Trindade
Rua Dr Justino Cúmano
A. de 5 Outubro
Rua Dr J. Lúcio
Praça da Liberdade
Rua do Bocage
IGREJA DE SÃO FRANCISCO
Rua de Portugal
Rua de Caçadores
TEATRO LETHES
Rua Cruz dos Mestres
Rua Vasco da Gama
R. de Santo António
CONVENTO DE NOSSA SENHORA DA ASSUNÇÃO
Rua do Alportel
Rua do Alportel
IGREJA DE SÃO PEDRO
Rua Frei L. de Santa Maria
Largo do Carmo
Rua José Estêvão
R. Filipe Alistão
ARCO DA VILA
Town Hall
CATEDRAL
R. do Compromisso
Praça Dr Francisco Gomes
Jardim Manuel Bivar
Bishop's Palace
Largo da Sé
Rua Frederico Lecor
IGREJA DO CARMO
Rua do Prior
Rua Serpa Pinto
R. Com. Francisco Manuel
Rua Manuel Ascensão
Rua Consel/heiro Bivar
Avenida da República
Rua Aboim Ascensão
Rua Infante Dom Henrique

Walk

Duration: 3 hr, excluding visits.

From the Manuel Bivar gardens beside the harbour, head for the Old Town, passing through the Arco da Vila (see **FARO-ATTRACTIONS**) into Rua do Município, a narrow, cobbled street that leads into Largo da Sé (see **FARO-ATTRACTIONS**). The Catedral (see **FARO-ATTRACTIONS**) is one of Faro's great tourist attractions, and the square houses the 18thC Bishop's Palace and the Town Hall. Beside the Town Hall on Rua Domingos Guieiro is Cidade Velha (see **FARO-RESTAURANTS**), one of the best restaurants in town. Rua Domingos Guieiro leads to Praça Afonso III and the Convento de Nossa Senhora da Assunção (see **FARO-ATTRACTIONS**) which contains the Museu Arqueológico Infante D. Henrique (see **FARO-MUSEUMS**). Follow Rua do Repouso beyond the old city walls into Rua de Teresa Ramalho Ortigão, then turn right into Rua de Caçadores. At the end of the street is the Igreja de São Francisco (see **FARO-ATTRACTIONS**). Retrace your steps along Rua de Caçadores and enter Praça Alexandre Herculano ahead on the right. On the corner of Praça da Liberdade is the District Assembly Building which contains the Museu Etnográfico Regional (see **FARO-MUSEUMS**). Cross the square and follow Rua de Portugal to the Teatro Lethes (see **FARO-MUSEUMS & CULTURE**), housed in a former Jesuit college. Follow Rua Dr Justino Crimano up the hill to the local market (in the large white building with a clock tower), bustling with people buying fresh fish and vegetables. At the market turn left and follow Rua General Teófilo Trindade, then turn left into Rua Horta Machado and follow Rua Cruz dos Mestres into Largo do Poço, which joins Largo de São Pedro, to visit the church of São Pedro. To the right is Largo do Carmo, and the Igreja do Carmo (see **FARO-ATTRACTIONS**), with its curious Capela dos Ossos, overlooking the square. From Largo de São Pedro, follow Rua Felipe Alistão into Praça Ferreira de Almeida, a lively square with some excellent restaurants. Follow Rua Vasco da Gama past the comic-looking bust of Dr Silva Nobre, then turn right into Rua de Santo António, the main shopping centre, which has been pedestrianized. Walk through the precinct into Praça Dr Francisco Gomes with its busy street cafés beside the Jardim Manuel Bivar, which is where you began.

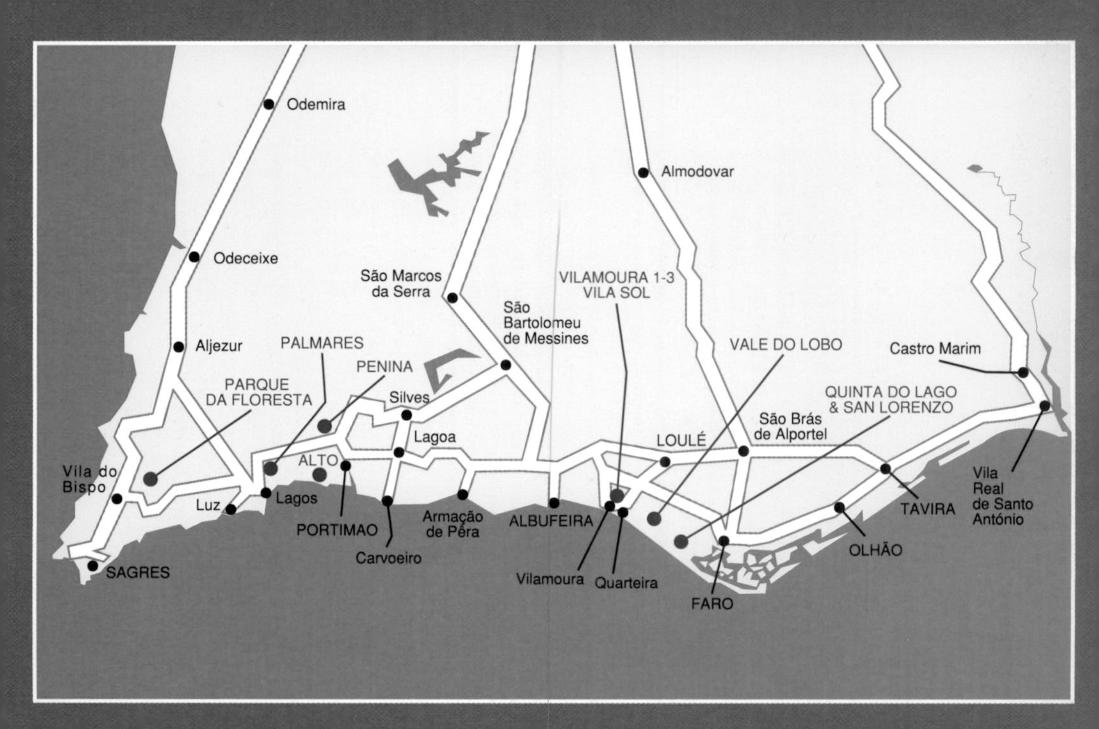

Odemira
Almodovar
Odeceixe
São Marcos da Serra
VILAMOURA 1-3 VILA SOL
São Bartolomeu de Messines
Aljezur
PALMARES
VALE DO LOBO
Castro Marim
PENINA
PARQUE DA FLORESTA
Silves
QUINTA DO LAGO & SAN LORENZO
São Brás de Alportel
Lagoa
LOULÉ
ALTO
Vila do Bispo
Lagos
Luz
Vila Real de Santo António
TAVIRA
Armação de Pêra
ALBUFEIRA
PORTIMAO
Carvoeiro
OLHÃO
SAGRES
Vilamoura
Quarteira
FARO

VILAMOURA 1-3 Marina de Vilamoura, 22 km east of Albufeira.
■ 0700-dusk. ● 6500 Esc. (1 & 2), 5000 Esc. (3).
Nos 1 & 2 were designed by Pennink. No. 1 is the most challenging of Vilamoura's courses, while the first nine holes of No. 2 lie along the coast and the return nine among the pine trees. No. 3, opened in 1990, is the easiest of Vilamoura's courses and has three nine-hole loops.

QUINTA DO LAGO & SAN LORENZO Quinta do Lago, 8 km from Faro. ■ 0730/0800-dusk. ● 10,000 Esc. (Q. do L.), 12,500 (S. L.).
Quinta do Lago is four separate nine-hole courses, the first three designed by W. Mitchell. There's a restaurant, pro shop, bar and showers. San Lorenzo is built around a large lake and has semi-island greens.

VALE DO LOBO 5 km from Almansil. ■ 0800-dusk. ● 10,000 Esc. per day (5000 Esc. after 1500).
Three courses (Red, Yellow and Green) designed by Henry Cotton. The Red course is particularly challenging.

PENINA Figueira, 5 km west of Portimão. ■ 0730-dusk. ● 9500 Esc.
This course, also designed by Henry Cotton, is famous for its 13th hole. A bar, pro shop and showers are inside the hotel.

PALMARES Meia Praia, 2 km from Lagos. ■ 0730-1930. ● 6000 Esc.
An 18-hole course renowned for its 15th hole. In Jan. the Almond Blossom contest is a great attraction.

PARQUE DA FLORESTA Vale do Poço, Budens, 16 km west of Lagos on the EN 125. ■ 0730-1800. ● 5500 Esc.
Designed by Pepe Gancedo. A varied and interesting course.

ALTO Alvor, 2 km west of Portimão. ■ 0730-dusk. ● 7000 Esc.
A new 18-hole course opened in 1991 and designed by Henry Cotton. The 604 m 16th is one of the longest par fives around.

VILA SOL 4 km from Vilamoura. ■ 0800-1830. ● 10,000 Esc.
A new, natural-style course with an elegant clubhouse.

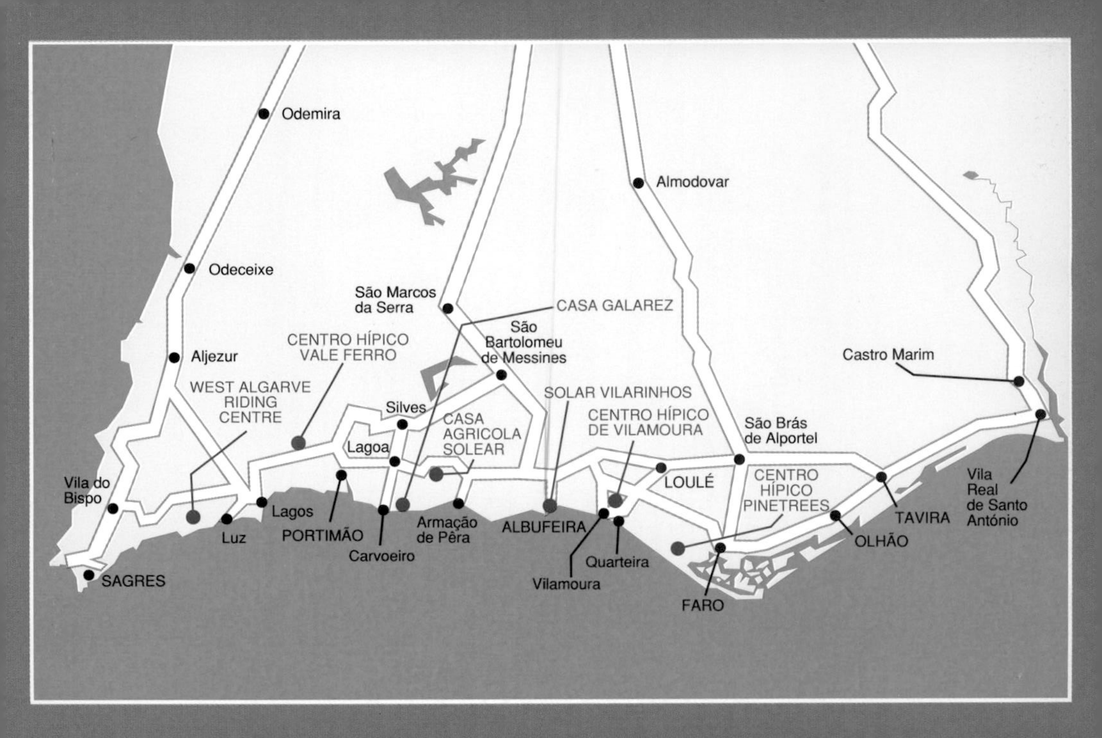
Odemira
Odeceixe
Aljezur
Almodovar
Castro Marim
São Marcos da Serra
São Bartolomeu de Messines
CASA GALAREZ
CENTRO HÍPICO VALE FERRO
WEST ALGARVE RIDING CENTRE
Silves
Lagoa
CASA AGRICOLA SOLEAR
SOLAR VILARINHOS
CENTRO HÍPICO DE VILAMOURA
São Brás de Alportel
LOULÉ
CENTRO HÍPICO PINETREES
Vila do Bispo
SAGRES
Luz
Lagos
PORTIMÃO
Carvoeiro
Armação de Pêra
ALBUFEIRA
Vilamoura
Quarteira
FARO
OLHÃO
TAVIRA
Vila Real de Santo António

Stables are usually open 0900-dusk. Expect to pay 3000-4000 Esc. per hr for trekking and 4000-6000 Esc. per hr for tuition.

WEST ALGARVE RIDING CENTRE
Burgau, 4 km west of Luz.
Shetland ponies for the kids. Bird-watching and flower-spotting trips, and day rides with a picnic lunch are also available.

CENTRO HÍPICO VALE FERRO
Mexhileira Grande, 10 km west of Portimão.
Beach and country trekking. Rides on ponies are also available for children over 7.

CASA GALAREZ
Lagoa, between Benagil and Carvoeiro.
Individual lessons and weekly packages, as well as ponies for children.

CASA AGRICOLA SOLEAR
Porches, 8 km east of Lagoa.
This centre has indoor and outdoor showjumping, and guided cross-country rides.

SOLAR VILARINHOS
Montechoro, Albufeira.
Country and beach rides. Tuition is available.

CENTRO HÍPICO DE VILAMOURA
Estalagem de Cegonha, Vilamoura.
Full-size stadium, track jumps and runs. Cross-country or beach rides for beginners and experienced riders.

CENTRO HÍPICO PINETREES
Quinta do Lago, 8 km south of Almansil.
Ponies for the kids, and qualified instructors speaking English, French and German. Recommended.

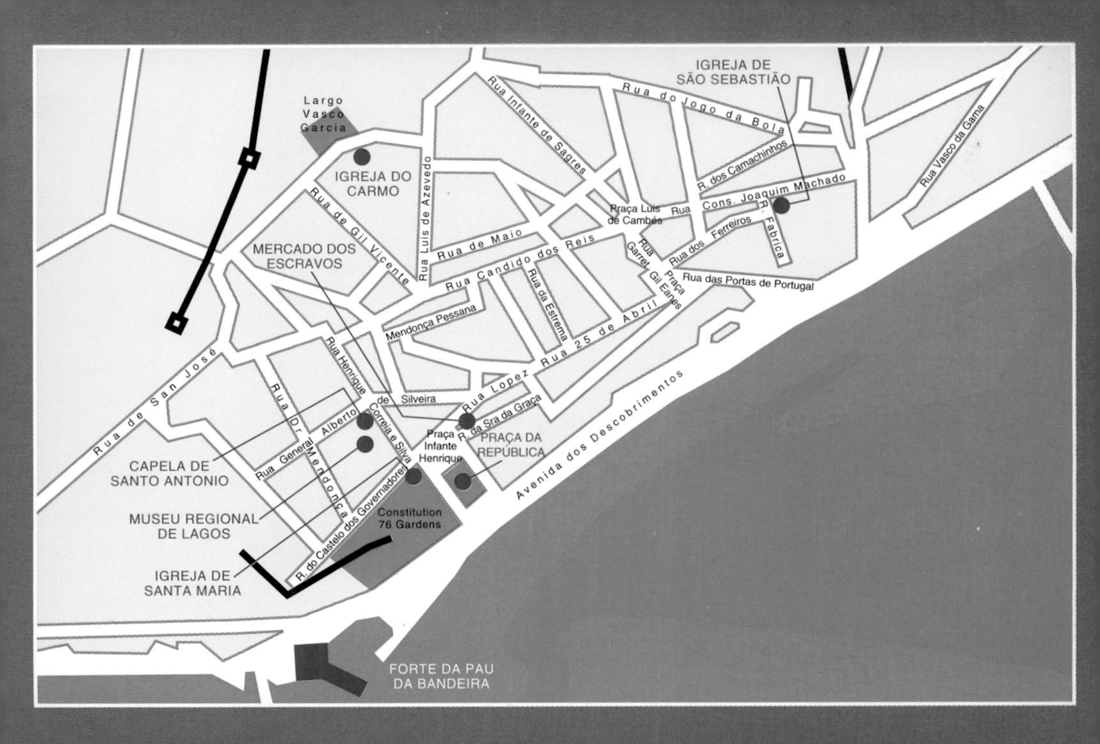

IGREJA DE SÃO SEBASTIÃO
Largo Vasco Garcia
IGREJA DO CARMO
Rua do Jogo da Bola
Rua Infante de Sagres
R. dos Camachinhos
Rua Cons. Joaquim Machado
Rua Vasco da Gama
Rua Luis de Azevedo
Rua de Gil Vicente
Rua de Maio
Praça Luis de Cambés
R. Fabrica
Rua dos Ferreiros
MERCADO DOS ESCRAVOS
Rua Candido dos Reis
Rua Garret
Praça Gil Eanes
Rua das Portas de Portugal
Rua da Estrema
Mendonça Pessana
Rua 25 de Abril
Rua de San José
Rua Henrique de Silveira
Rua Lopez
Rua Dr Mendonça
Rua General Alberto
Correia e Silva
R. da Sra da Graça
Praça Infante Henrique
PRAÇA DA REPÚBLICA
Avenida dos Descobrimentos
CAPELA DE SANTO ANTONIO
MUSEU REGIONAL DE LAGOS
R. do Castelo dos Governadores
Constitution 76 Gardens
IGREJA DE SANTA MARIA
FORTE DA PAU DA BANDEIRA

CAPELA DE SANTO ANTÓNIO
Rua General de Alberto Silveira, next door to the Museu Regional de Lagos (see below).
Has a lavishly gilded Baroque nave and a talha dourada *(see* **A-Z***) altar.*

MUSEU REGIONAL DE LAGOS
Rua General de Alberto Silveira. The museum can be entered from the Capela de Santo António (see above).
■ 0930-1230, 1400-1700 Wed.-Mon. Closed hols. ● Inexpensive.
A varied collection illustrating the history of the local peasantry.

PRAÇA DA REPÚBLICA
Henry the Navigator's (see **A-Z***) statue sits in the centre of the square. Note the Baroque façade of the Igreja de Santa Maria (see below), and the Mercado dos Escravos (see below).*

IGREJA DE SÃO SEBASTIÃO
Rua Conselheiro Joaquim Machado.
On the outside there are attractive Renaissance gates, and on the inside precious 17th and 18thC azulejos *(see* **A-Z***).*

IGREJA DE SANTA MARIA Praça da República.
Built in Renaissance style and restored in the 19thC. Houses fine statues.

IGREJA DO CARMO Largo Vasco Garcia.
Along Rua Marreiros from the tourist office.
Ruined church with 18thC azulejos *(tiles) and examples of* talha dourada.

MERCADO DOS ESCRAVOS
Praça da República. At the top of the square on the right.
A small area enclosed by railings marks the site where slaves were auctioned for the first time in Portugal.

FORTE DA PAU DA BANDEIRA Avenida dos Descobrimentos.
● Inexpensive.
A small 17thC fort guarding the harbour entrance. Houses a museum.

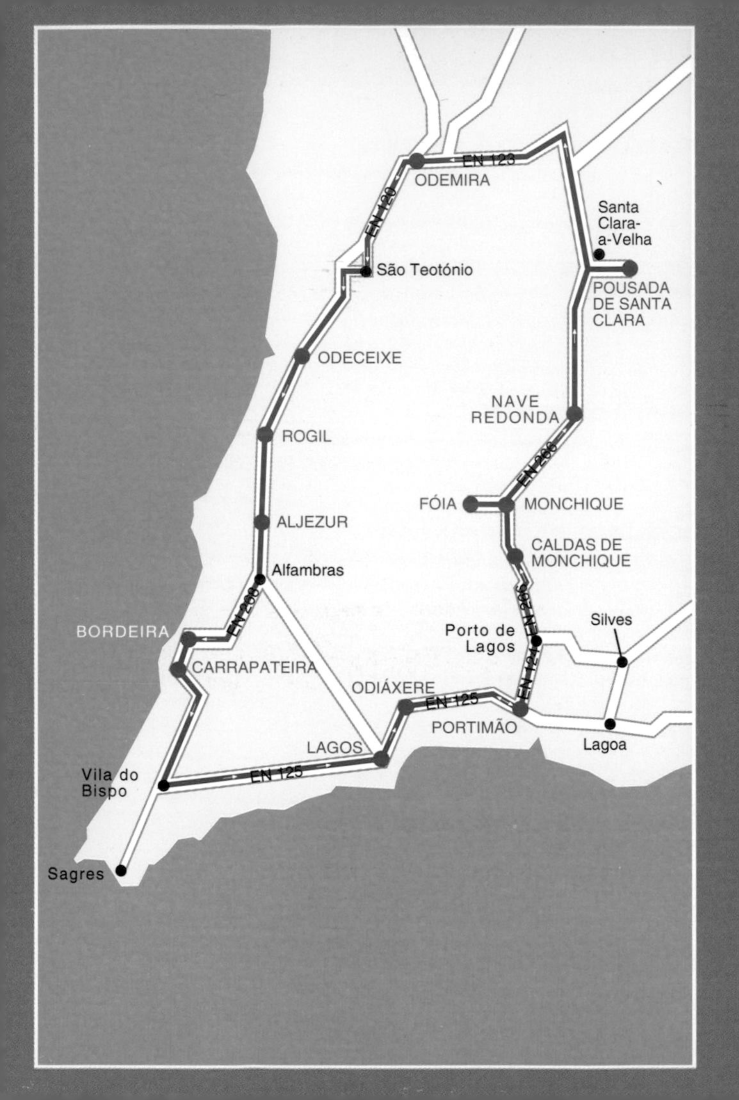
EN 123
ODEMIRA
EN 120
Santa
Clara-
a-Velha
São Teotónio
POUSADA
DE SANTA
CLARA
ODECEIXE
NAVE
REDONDA
ROGIL
EN 266
FÓIA
MONCHIQUE
ALJEZUR
CALDAS DE
MONCHIQUE
Alfambras
EN 268
EN 266
Silves
BORDEIRA
Porto de
Lagos
CARRAPATEIRA
EN 124
ODIÁXERE
EN 125
PORTIMÃO
Lagoa
LAGOS
Vila do
Bispo
EN 125
Sagres

Excursion 1

A one- or two-day excursion through the hills of the Algarve, the forests of Monchique, and down to the beaches of the Atlantic coast.

Leave Lagos on the EN 125 to Portimão.
5 km – Odiáxere. There is a late-18thC church with a Manueline (see **A-Z**) portal built of red sandstone here. Continue to Portimão (see **PORTIMÃO**, **A-Z**). Retrace your route a short distance then turn right along the EN 124 towards Silves. Fork left again after Porto de Lagos (7 km) onto the EN 266 towards Monchique.
36 km – Caldas de Monchique. The waters here are said to possess life-prolonging properties but there is one drawback – they smell disgusting! Above Caldas de Monchique the road winds uphill to Monchique, giving wide views of the area.
44 km – Monchique (see **A-Z**). Two kilometres from Monchique on the EN 266-3 leading to Fóia, you can stop for a meal (or spend the night after a walk on the mountain) at the Abrigo da Montanha, a superb mountain inn set among flowers and ferns.
56 km – Fóia. At 902 m, this is the highest point in the Algarve. The road winds uphill through eucalyptus and pine trees which thin out towards the top. From here you can enjoy an unimpeded outlook over the whole of southern Portugal (unless the weather turns misty, which is not unusual in summer). Return to Monchique and take the EN 266 towards Aljustrel. The route slopes gently down through the forest.
66 km – Nave Redonda. The gateway to the plains of Alentejo. After 14 km, on the right is the road to the lake and dam of Santa Clara. A local *pousada* (Pousada de Santa Clara at Santa Clara-a-Velha) has a picnic and barbecue area which overlooks one of the loveliest lake settings in Portugal. Return to the main road and after another 11 km turn left onto the EN 123.
108 km – Odemira. A quiet little village tucked into a bend of the Mira river. Turn left onto the EN 120. Drive towards São Teotónio, turning right onto the EN 120 for Aljezur. Continue for 10 km beyond São Teotónio.
122 km – Odeceixe. A pretty village in typical surroundings. The road winds uphill and then descends through eucalyptus trees.
132 km – Rogil. To the right is the rough track to Estreira and the beach

Lagos

of Samouqueira. You will need a 4-wheel drive vehicle to negotiate the tracks in this area.
140 km – Aljezur. A pleasant town with the ruins of a Moorish fortress. At Alfambras continue straight on, following the signs for Sagres, then turn right onto the EN 268 for Vila do Bispo.
161 km – Carrapateira. A small village among the sands. The beaches of Bordeira and Carrapateira are becoming popular with surfers. Note that the tracks around here can be very difficult to drive on. Continue for 14 km to Vila do Bispo, then take the EN 125 to return to Lagos (200 km).

Mouranitos
Barriga
Cordama
Castelejo
EM 1256
NOSSA SENHORA
DO GUADALOUPE
RAPOSEIRA
VILA DO BISPO
EM 1256
GRUTAS DO
MONTE FRANCES
FORTE
DO
BELICHE
EN 268
CABO
DE SÃO
VICENTE
SAGRES
BUDENS
EN 125
BURGAU
SALEMA
RM 537
PRAIA DA LUZ
Quatro
Estradas
LAGOS
Odiáxere

Excursion 2

A one-day excursion from Lagos to the 'World's End'.

Leave Lagos on the EN 125 for Vila do Bispo. After 5 km, at Quatro Estradas, turn left onto the RM 537.
8 km – Praia da Luz (see **BEACHES 1**). A large, pleasant beach stretching beneath the cliffs. Climb up to the Mirador de Atalaia on your left. In the distance, to the west, is Cabo de São Vicente. Follow the coast road (RM 537) to Burgau.
12 km – Burgau (see **BEACHES 1**). Return to the EN 125.
22 km – Budens. The village has a Baroque chapel. Leave on the EN 125 for Vila do Bispo. Two kilometres further on is the turning to Salema, a fishing village with an attractive beach (see **BEACHES 1**). Return to the EN 125.
28 km – Nossa Senhora do Guadaloupe. On the right, watch out for this 13thC Gothic chapel where Henry the Navigator (see **A-Z**) prayed.
30 km – Raposeira. Henry the Navigator lived in a *quinta* here and surrounded himself with the best geographers, astronomers and cartographers of the time to help him plan the great voyages of exploration.
32 km – Vila do Bispo. If you can get in, visit the Baroque church, which is decorated with 18thC *azulejos* (see **A-Z**), and has a *talha dourada* (see **A-Z**) altar. Turn left onto the EN 268 to Sagres.
39 km – Monte Frances Caves. The main entrance is on the left.
42 km – Sagres (see **A-Z**). At the crossroads in Sagres take the EN 268 to Cabo de São Vicente. The road follows a bleak, storm-lashed plateau and offers breathtaking views.
49 km – Forte do Beliche. This small fort before the lighthouse now houses a restaurant and outstation for the *pousada* in Sagres.
50 km – Cabo de São Vincente. Known as 'World's End' or 'O Fim do Mundo'. It is worth spending some time contemplating the spectacular panorama from this spot. Sunsets viewed from here are particularly impressive. Return to Sagres and retrace your route to Vila do Bispo. From here head west to the beaches of Castelejo, Cordama, Barriga and Mouranitos (see **BEACHES 1**), and the Mirador Torre de Aspa, or visit the safer and more sheltered beaches of Sagres (Tonel and Mareta on either side of Sagres promontory). Return on the EN 125 to Lagos (110 km).

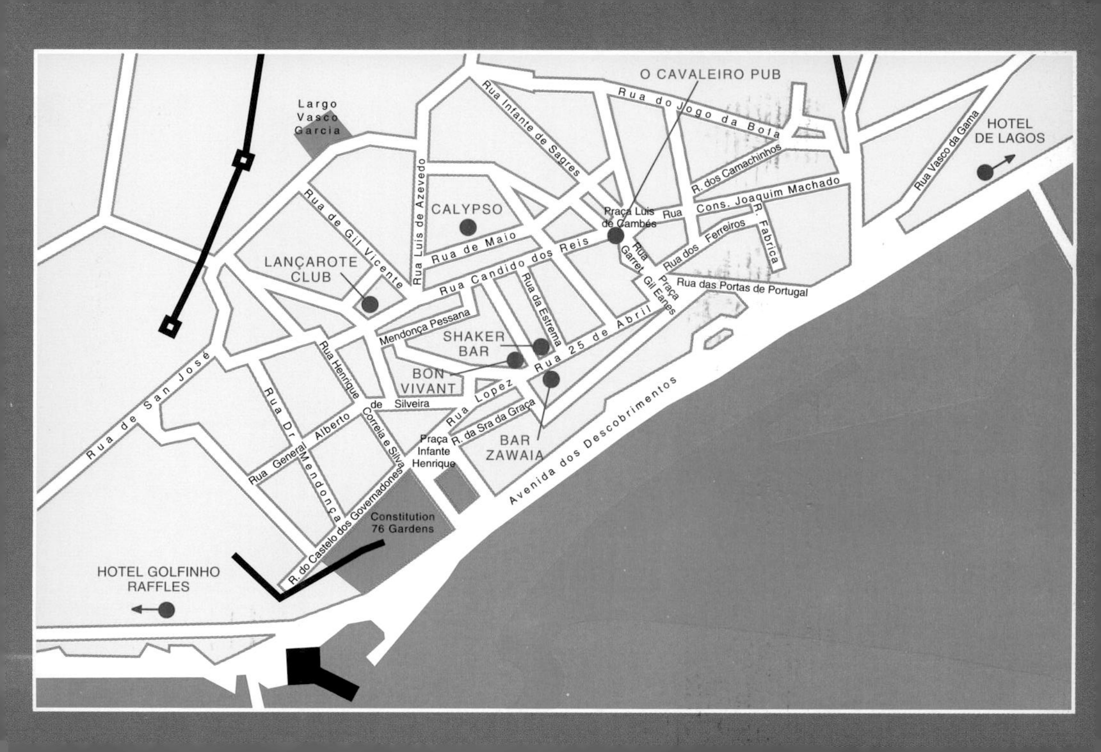
O CAVALEIRO PUB
Largo Vasco Garcia
Rua Infante de Sagres
Rua do Jogo da Bola
HOTEL DE LAGOS
Rua Vasco da Gama
R. dos Camachinhos
Rua Cons. Joaquim Machado
R. Fabrica
Rua dos Ferreiros
Praça Luis de Cambés
CALYPSO
Rua Luis de Azevedo
Rua de Gil Vicente
Rua de Maio
Rua Candido dos Reis
Rua Garret
Praça Gil Eanes
Rua das Portas de Portugal
LANÇAROTE CLUB
Mendonça Pessana
Rua da Estrema
SHAKER BAR
Rua 25 de Abril
BON VIVANT
Rua Henrique de Silveira
Rua Lopez
Rua de San José
Rua Dr Alberto
Correia e Silva
R. da Sra da Graça
Praça Infante Henrique
BAR ZAWAIA
Avenida dos Descobrimentos
Rua General Mendonça
R. do Castelo dos Governadones
Constitution 76 Gardens
HOTEL GOLFINHO RAFFLES

See **Opening Times**.

Catch the mournful traditional singing and the happy, whirling folk dancing of Portugal at Hotel de Lagos and Hotel Golfinho. Enquire at the tourist office for details of days and times. See **Fado**.

LANÇAROTE CLUB
Rua Lançarote de Freitas 26.
A successful combination of restaurant, bar and discotheque.

BON VIVANT
Rua 25 de Abril 105.
A very popular disco on three levels, with panoramic views from the terrace.

BAR ZAWAIA
Rua 25 de Abril 99.
A bar popular with all nationalities, which offers exotic cocktails.

O CAVALEIRO PUB
Rua Garret 23.
Open all day long (and late into the night) for a drink or a snack.

SHAKER BAR
Rua 25 de Abril 68.
Popular with young locals but everyone is made welcome.

RAFFLES
Edifício Luz Tur, Praia da Luz.
Delicious cocktails can be sipped in perfect surroundings on the lovely beach (see **BEACHES 1***).*

CALYPSO
Rua de Maio 22.
A club with lots of character and rock music.

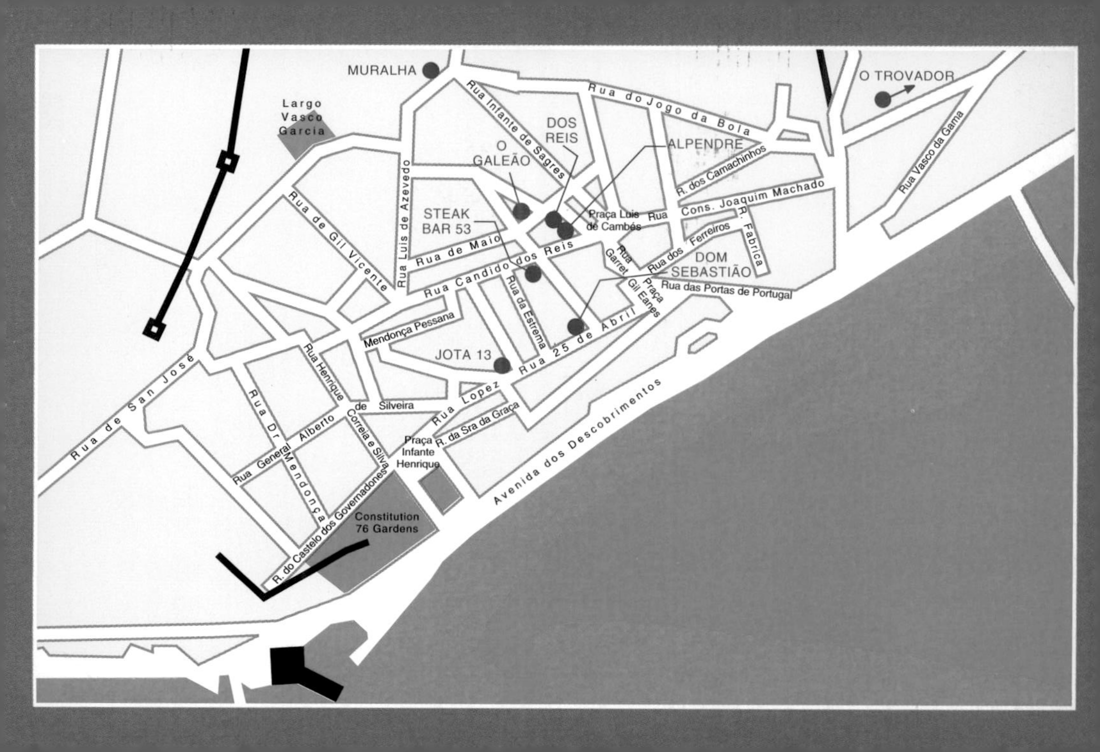
MURALHA
O TROVADOR
Largo Vasco Garcia
Rua do Jogo da Bola
Rua Infante de Sagres
DOS REIS
O GALEÃO
ALPENDRE
R. dos Camachinhos
Rua Cons. Joaquim Machado
Rua Vasco da Gama
STEAK BAR 53
Praça Luis de Cambés
Rua de Gil Vicente
Rua Luis de Azevedo
Rua de Maio
Rua Candido dos Reis
Rua Garret
Rua dos Ferreiros
R. Fabrica
DOM SEBASTIÃO
Rua das Portas de Portugal
Praça Gil Eanes
Rua da Estrema
Mendonça Pessana
JOTA 13
Rua 25 de Abril
Rua de San José
Rua Henrique de Silveira
Rua Lopez
R. da Sra da Graça
Praça Infante Henrique
Rua Dr Alberto
Rua General Mendonça
Correia e Silva
R. do Castelo dos Governadores
Constitution 76 Gardens
Avenida dos Descobrimentos

See **Opening Times**.

DOM SEBASTIÃO Rua 25 de Abril 20.
● Expensive.
Excellent local and international food served in a delightful dining room.

ALPENDRE Rua António Barbosa Viana.
● Expensive.
Traditional Portuguese fare in a traditional setting.

DOS REIS Rua António Barbosa Viana 21.
● Moderate.
A limited, albeit excellent, selection of Portuguese specialities.

MURALHA Rua da Atalaia 15.
● Moderate.
Portuguese specialities are served here to the sound of Fado (see **A-Z***).*

O TROVADOR Largo Convento Senhora Glor.
■ Closed Sun. & Mon. ● Moderate.
Local and international food presented in a friendly atmosphere. British-owned establishment.

O GALEÃO Rua da Laranjeira 1.
■ Closed Sun. ● Moderate.
Good food, friendly service, an open kitchen, a bar and an intimate atmosphere. Reservations are recommended.

JOTA 13 Rua 25 de Abril 58.
● Moderate.
Favoured by the locals for its generous helpings of traditional food.

STEAK BAR 53 Rua Cândido dos Reis 53-55.
● Inexpensive.
Excellent grills and breakfasts (all English-style) served on a flower-decked patio.

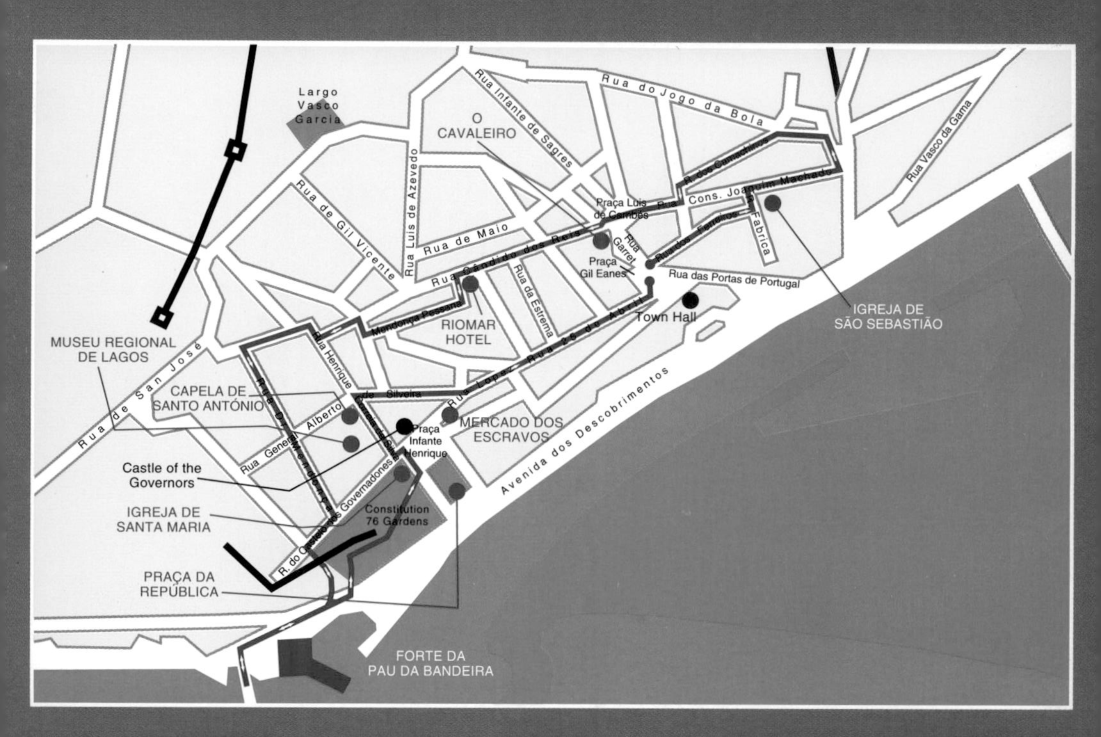

Largo Vasco Garcia
O CAVALEIRO
Rua Infante de Sagres
Rua do Jogo da Bola
Rua Vasco da Gama
R. dos Camachinos
Cons. Joaquim Machado
Rua Luis de Azevedo
Rua de Gil Vicente
Rua de Maio
Rua Cândido dos Reis
Praça Luis de Camões
Rua Garret
Praça Gil Eanes
Rua dos Ferreiros
Fabrica
Rua das Portas de Portugal
IGREJA DE SÃO SEBASTIÃO
Town Hall
Rua da Estrema
Rua 25 de Abril
RIOMAR HOTEL
Mendonça Pessana
MUSEU REGIONAL DE LAGOS
Rua de San José
Rua Henrique
de Silveira
Rua Lopez
CAPELA DE SANTO ANTÓNIO
Alberto
Rua General
Praça Infante Henrique
MERCADO DOS ESCRAVOS
Avenida dos Descobrimentos
Castle of the Governors
Rua Dr. Mendonça
Correia da Silva
Governadones
IGREJA DE SANTA MARIA
Constitution 76 Gardens
R. do Castelo dos Governadones
PRAÇA DA REPÚBLICA
FORTE DA PAU DA BANDEIRA

Walk

Duration: 2 hr.
Start from Praça Gil Eanes, the main square, home to the curious statue of King Sebastião with its flesh-coloured face. Leave the square on Rua Dos Ferreiros which climbs steeply up to the Igreja de São Sebastião (see **LAGOS-ATTRACTIONS**). Follow Rua Conselheiro Joaquim Machado. At the end of the road is a wall where you can look over the harbour to the right and along the coastline to the east of the town. To the left are fragments of the old city walls. Follow Rua da Torinha to the left down the hill into Rua dos Camachinos, then left onto Rua Dr António José de Almeida and right into Praça Luis de Cambés with its war memorial. On the corner of the square is O Cavaleiro (see **LAGOS-NIGHTLIFE**), a busy café/bar popular with locals and tourists for watching passers-by. Walk up Rua Cândido dos Reis, a busy shopping street, turn left past the Riomar Hotel into Mendonça Pessana and walk down the hill and across the Travessa do Cotovelo. Turn right then left into Rua 5 da Outubro, then walk up the hill and turn left into Rua Dr Mendonça, following the road to the junction with Rua do Castelo dos Governadores. Turn right then left through the archway beneath the old city walls. Across the road is the Forte da Pau da Bandeira (see **LAGOS-ATTRACTIONS**). Past the fort on the left, a strip of land leads out to a small light which marks the entrance to the harbour. From here you can see the coast to the east of Lagos, and also look back to the town. Head back into town past the fort and cross the road back into the Constitution 76 gardens. Follow the path with the old city walls to your left. Ahead is Praça da República (see **LAGOS-ATTRACTIONS**), with the statue of Henry the Navigator (see **A-Z**) gazing impassively out to sea. On the left of the square is the Igreja de Santa Maria (see **LAGOS-ATTRACTIONS**). On the opposite corner is the Mercado dos Escravos (see **LAGOS-ATTRACTIONS**). At the top of the square is the Castle of the Governors, which is often used to house the exhibitions of local artists. From the square follow Rua Henrique Correia de Silva. On the left is the Museu Regional de Lagos (see **LAGOS-ATTRACTIONS**) and beside it the Capela de Santo António (see **LAGOS-ATTRACTIONS**). Turn right into Rua Silva Lopez, which leads into Rua 25 de Abril, boasting lots of good eating places and bars. At the bottom of the street is Praça Gil Eanes where the walk began.

Portimão

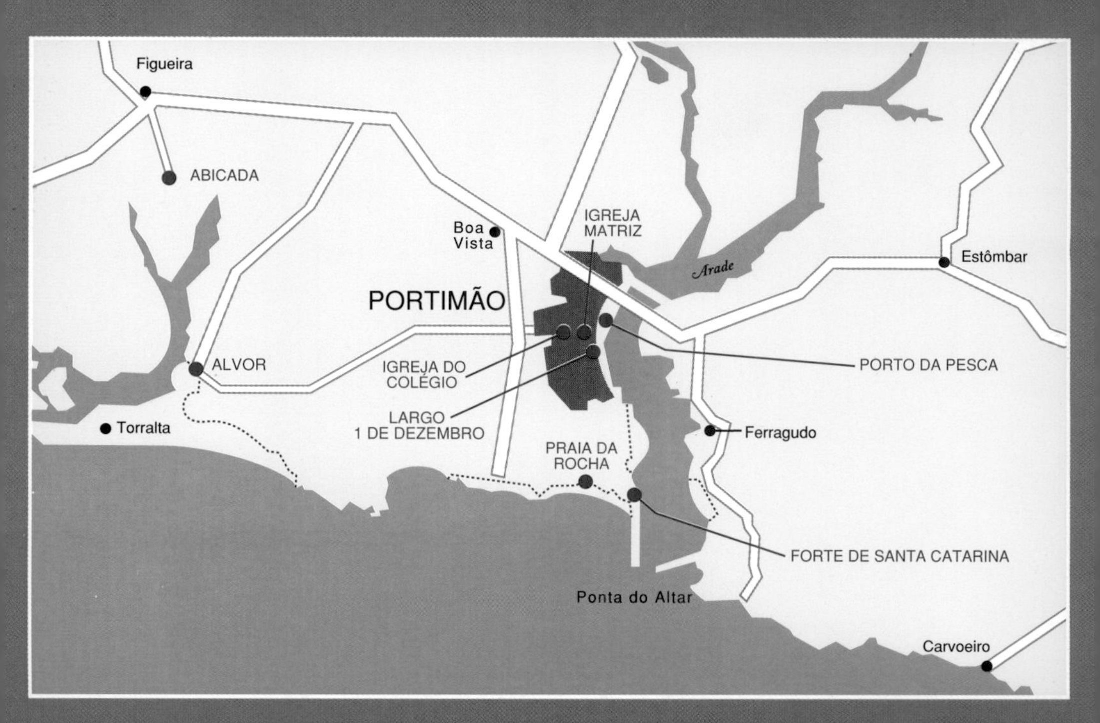
Figueira
ABICADA
Boa Vista
PORTIMÃO
IGREJA MATRIZ
Arade
Estômbar
ALVOR
IGREJA DO COLÉGIO
PORTO DA PESCA
LARGO 1 DE DEZEMBRO
Torralta
Ferragudo
PRAIA DA ROCHA
FORTE DE SANTA CATARINA
Ponta do Altar
Carvoeiro

PORTO DA PESCA (FISHING HARBOUR)
The sardine catch is now unloaded further down river but the old harbour is still full of atmosphere and well worth visiting for its good basic dockside restaurants and its many boat excursions.

IGREJA DO COLÉGIO
Praça da República.
Chapel of Jesuit college, with polychromatic marbles and 17thC piedade.

IGREJA MATRIZ
Rua Diogo Tomé. Along Rua Cabrita from Largo 1 de Dezembro.
A large Baroque church with Gothic gates and 17thC azulejos *(see* **A-Z***).*

LARGO 1 DE DEZEMBRO
A small park containing ornamental benches with azulejo *(tile) panels portraying important episodes from Portugal's history.*

PRAIA DA ROCHA
4 km south of Portimão.
A 1 hr walk along the cliffs from Forte de Santa Catarina (see below) to the Mirador João de Arens. There are splendid views of the beach and coastline. See BEACHES 2.

FORTE DE SANTA CATARINA
At east end of Praia da Rocha.
A 16thC fort which, along with its twin on the opposite bank in Ferragudo, once guarded the estuary of the river Arade.

ALVOR
On the EM 531-1 6 km west of Portimão.
A popular seaside resort above a charming fishing village containing an attractive 18thC church with a Manueline (see **A-Z***) portal.*

ABICADA
On the EN 125 7 km west of Portimão.
■ Closed in the early evening.
Close to a lagoon, these are the ruins of an opulent 4thC Roman villa.

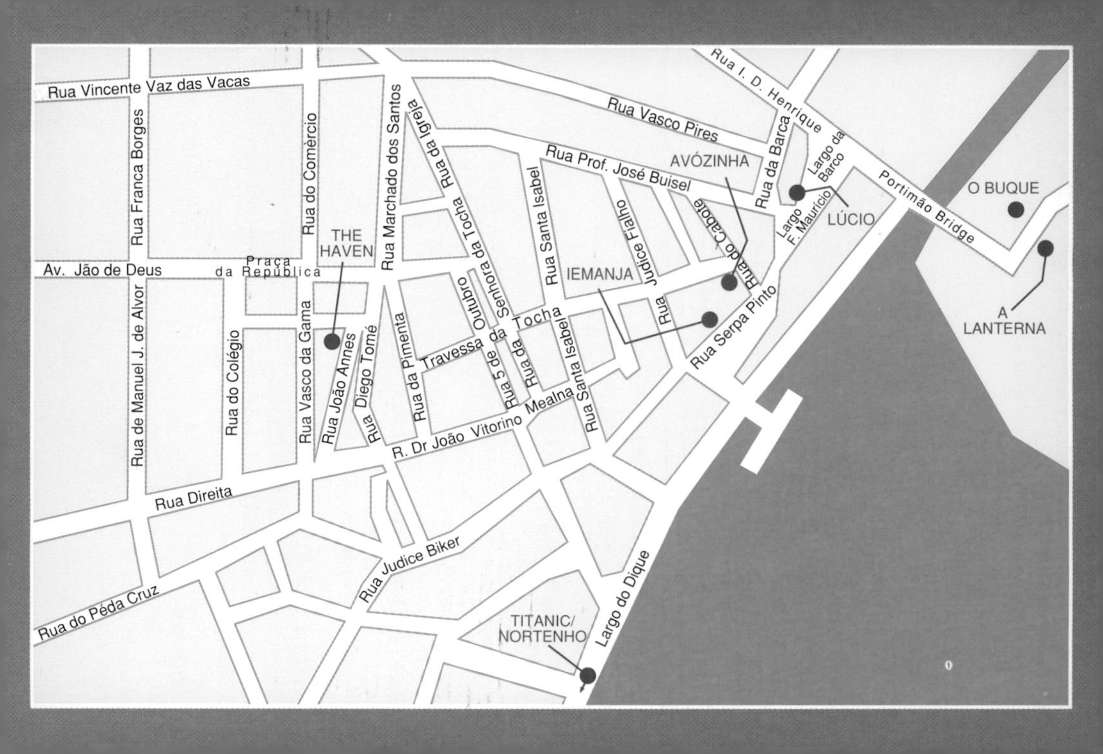
Rua Vincente Vaz das Vacas
Rua Franca Borges
Rua do Comércio
THE HAVEN
Rua Marchado dos Santos
Rua da Igreja
Senhora da Tocha
Rua Santa Isabel
Rua Vasco Pires
Rua I. D. Henrique
Rua Prof. José Buisel
AVÓZINHA
Rua da Barca
Largo da Barco
LÚCIO
Largo F. Maurício
Portimão Bridge
O BUQUE
A LANTERNA
Rua do Cabote
Rua Judice Fialho
IEMANJA
Rua Serpa Pinto
Av. Jão de Deus
Praça da República
Rua de Manuel J. de Alvor
Rua do Colégio
Rua Vasco da Gama
Rua João Annes
Rua Diego Tomé
Rua da Pimenta
Travessa da Tocha
Outubro
Rua 5 de
Rua da
Mealna
Rua Santa Isabel
R. Dr João Vitorino
Rua Direita
Rua Judice Biker
Rua do Péda Cruz
TITANIC/ NORTENHO
Largo do Dique

Restaurants

See **Opening Times**.

IEMANJA Rua Serpa Pinto 9.
● Moderate-Expensive.
The unusual frontage hides some of the best Portuguese food in Portimão.

AVÓZINHA Rua do Cabote.
● Moderate-Expensive.
Small seafood restaurant with first-class service and warm atmosphere.

THE HAVEN Rua João Annes 35.
● Moderate.
Run by a Scottish couple who learnt the trade in one of Glasgow's top restaurants, there's good British food in this small, friendly eatery.

LÚCIO Largo F. Maurício. Near the Portimão bridge.
● Inexpensive.
Favoured by locals and tourists alike for its excellent seafood.

A LANTERNA Parchal. On the Ferragudo side of the Portimão bridge. ● Expensive.
Excellent fresh fish and duck.

O BUQUE Parchal. On the Ferragudo side of the Portimão bridge.
● Moderate-Expensive.
Wonderful seafood and steaks. Excellent service.

TITANIC Edifício Columbia, Praia da Rocha. Round the corner from the Jupiter Hotel. ● Moderate-Expensive.
Plush restaurant serving excellent Portuguese cuisine. Nightly musical entertainment and dancing in the Babylon Bar.

NORTENHO Praia da Rocha. Beside the tourist office.
● Inexpensive.
A favourite with British tourists. Everyone is made welcome by the Portuguese owner.

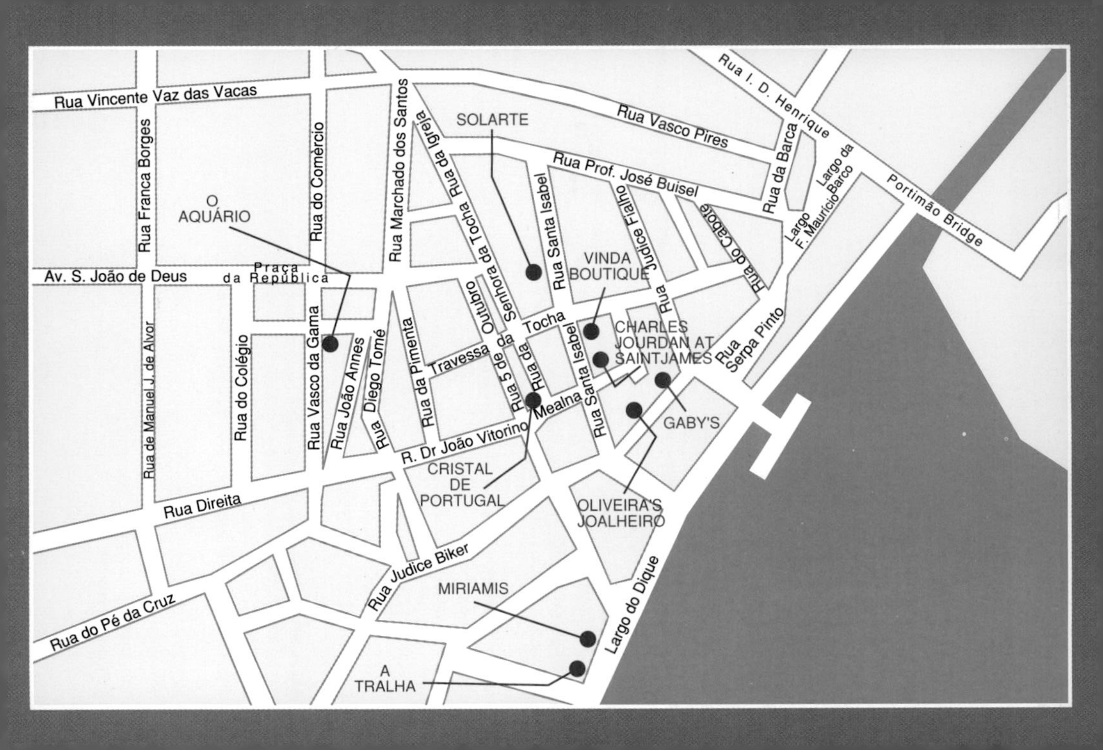

Rua Vincente Vaz das Vacas
Rua Vasco Pires
Rua I. D. Henrique
SOLARTE
Rua Franca Borges
Rua do Comércio
Rua Marchado dos Santos
Rua da Igreja
Rua Prof. José Buisel
Rua da Barca
Largo da Barco
Largo F. Maurício
Portimão Bridge
O AQUÁRIO
Rua Senhora da Tocha
Rua Santa Isabel
Rua Judice Fialho
Rua do Caboie
VINDA BOUTIQUE
Av. S. João de Deus
Praça da República
Outubro
Rua 5 de
Travessa da Tocha
Rua da Mealna
Rua Santa Isabel
CHARLES JOURDAN AT SAINTJAMES
Rua
Rua Serpa Pinto
Rua de Manuel J. de Alvor
Rua do Colégio
Rua Vasco da Gama
Rua João Annes
Rua Diego Tomé
Rua da Pimenta
R. Dr João Vitorino
GABY'S
CRISTAL DE PORTUGAL
OLIVEIRA'S JOALHEIRO
Rua Direita
Rua Judice Biker
Largo do Dique
MIRIAMIS
Rua do Pé da Cruz
A TRALHA

Shopping

See **Opening Times**.

VINDA BOUTIQUE Rua Santa Isabel 32.
Handmade gifts, including china, ceramics, leather goods, pewter and embroidery.

CRISTAL DE PORTUGAL Rua 5 de Outubro 16a.
One of the few shops in the Algarve where you can still find genuine hand-engraved crystal.

MIRIAMIS Largo do Dique 11.
A complete selection of Algarvian handicrafts at moderate prices.

SOLARTE Rua Santa Isabel 56.
A large selection of Portuguese handicrafts.

O AQUÁRIO
On Praça da República & Rua Vasco da Gama corner. There's also a branch on Rua Direita.
Crystal, ceramics, pottery, china, pewter and copper articles.

GABY'S Praça Visconde Bivar 15.
Specialist in fine leathers and Madeira embroideries.

A TRALHA Largo do Dique 15.
It is possible to come across genuine finds among the local antiques sold here. There is another branch in Albufeira.

CHARLES JOURDAN AT SAINT JAMES Rua Santa Isabel 26.
One of the best shoemakers in the Algarve. Made-to-measure items are available at moderate prices.

OLIVEIRA'S JOALHEIRO Praça Visconde Bivar.
Silver and goldsmith's shop especially good for filigree and silverware.

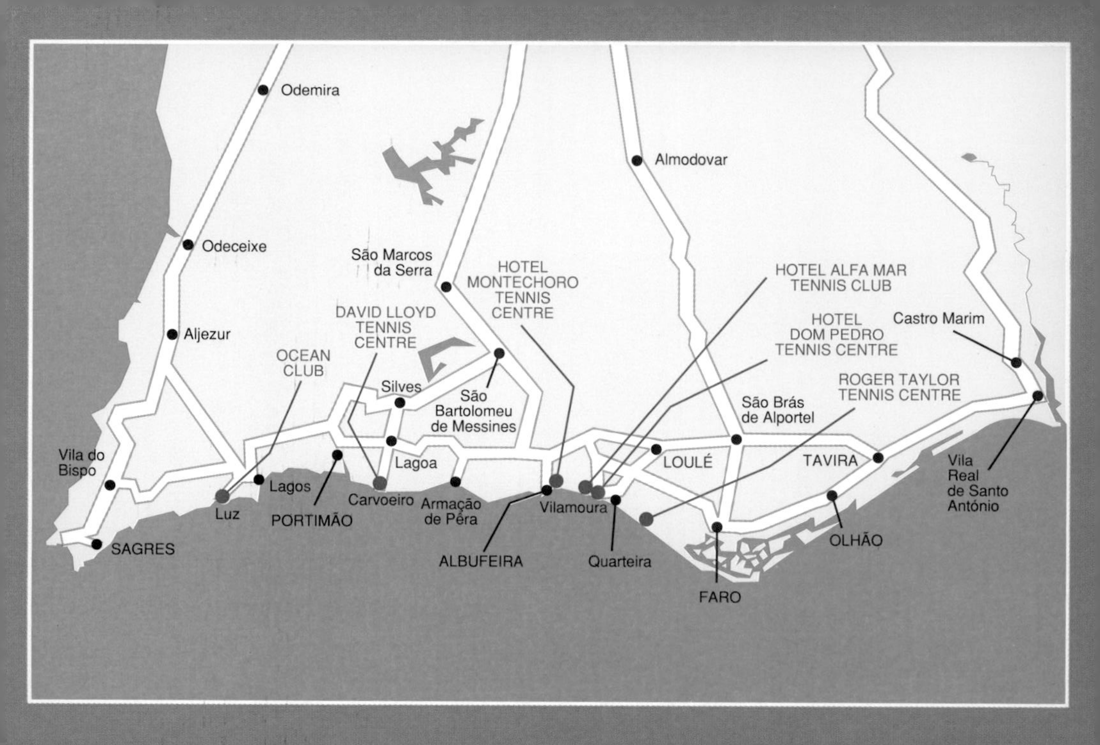
Odemira
Almodovar
Odeceixe
São Marcos da Serra
HOTEL MONTECHORO TENNIS CENTRE
HOTEL ALFA MAR TENNIS CLUB
Aljezur
DAVID LLOYD TENNIS CENTRE
HOTEL DOM PEDRO TENNIS CENTRE
Castro Marim
OCEAN CLUB
Silves
São Bartolomeu de Messines
ROGER TAYLOR TENNIS CENTRE
São Brás de Alportel
Vila do Bispo
Lagoa
LOULÉ
TAVIRA
Vila Real de Santo António
Lagos
Luz
Carvoeiro
Armação de Pêra
Vilamoura
PORTIMÃO
SAGRES
ALBUFEIRA
Quarteira
OLHÃO
FARO

Expect to pay 1000-3000 Esc. per hr for a court and 2500-5000 Esc. per hr for a lesson.

OCEAN CLUB

Praia da Luz.
Offers first-class tennis coaching in one of the coast's most successful tourist developments.

DAVID LLOYD TENNIS CENTRE

Rocha Brava, Carvoeiro.
The centre has ten tennis courts and two squash courts. Tennis coaching and video analysis are available.

HOTEL MONTECHORO TENNIS CENTRE

Montechoro, east of Albufeira.
Ten courts in one of the new tourist developments overlooking the sea. Also has squash courts.

HOTEL ALFA MAR TENNIS CLUB

Praia da Falésia, 10 km east of Albufeira.
Has 18 courts. Major Algarvian tournaments are often held here.

HOTEL DOM PEDRO TENNIS CENTRE

Marina de Vilamoura.
There are three courts and equipment is available for hire. An international tournament is held here during the annual Almond Blossom festival.

ROGER TAYLOR TENNIS CENTRE

Vale do Lobo, south of Almansil.
One of Europe's leading tennis centres, with no fewer than 21 courts. Equipment can be hired and lessons are available. Day visitors can use the courts; enquire at reception.

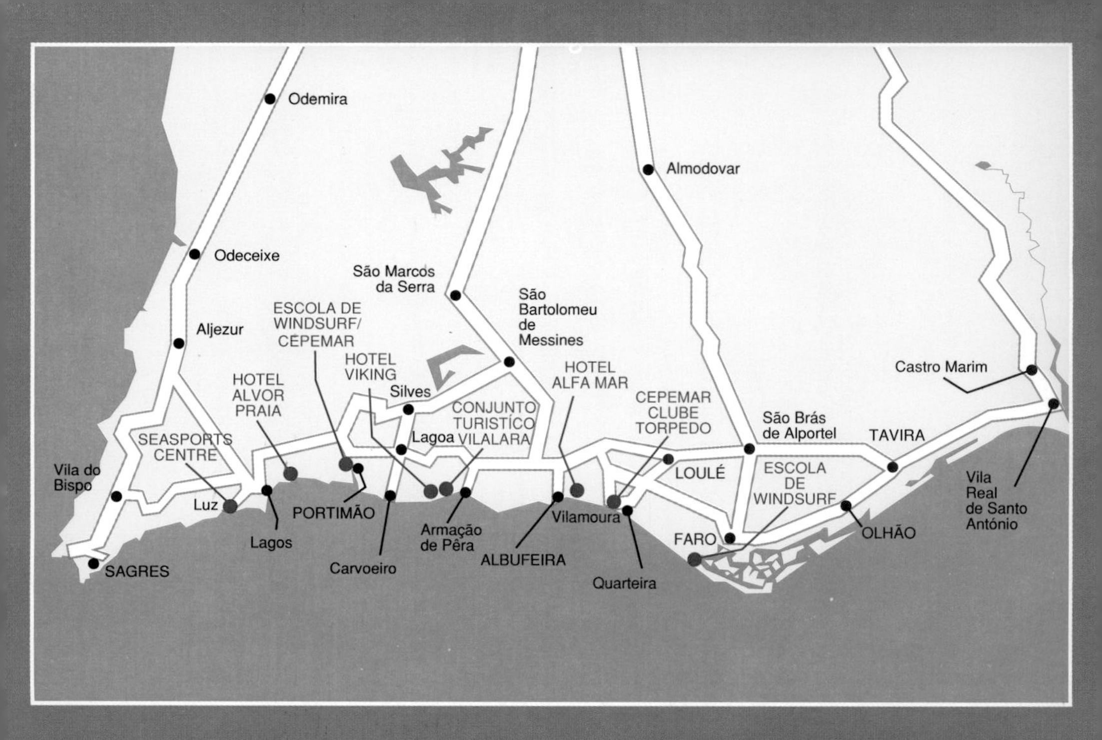
Odemira
Almodovar
Odeceixe
São Marcos da Serra
São Bartolomeu de Messines
Aljezur
ESCOLA DE WINDSURF/ CEPEMAR
HOTEL VIKING
HOTEL ALVOR PRAIA
Silves
HOTEL ALFA MAR
CEPEMAR CLUBE TORPEDO
São Brás de Alportel
Castro Marim
SEASPORTS CENTRE
CONJUNTO TURISTÍCO VILALARA
Lagoa
TAVIRA
Vila do Bispo
LOULÉ
ESCOLA DE WINDSURF
Luz
PORTIMÃO
Vilamoura
Vila Real de Santo António
Lagos
Armação de Pêra
FARO
OLHÃO
SAGRES
Carvoeiro
ALBUFEIRA
Quarteira

Expect to pay 5000-6000 Esc. per hr, including tuition, for sailing and windsurfing, and 5000-7500 Esc. per session for water-skiing.

SEASPORTS CENTRE Avenida dos Pescadores, Praia da Luz.
The longest-licensed scuba-diving centre in Portugal. Also offers fishing and big-game fishing.

HOTEL ALVOR PRAIA Praia dos Três Irmãos, Alvor.
Boat hire (for parties of 12), and deep-sea fishing equipment hire.

ESCOLA DE WINDSURF Praia da Rocha, Portimão, in front of the Hotel Algarve.
Board hire and lessons.

CEPEMAR Centro de Pesca Desportiva, Portimão, and Marina de Vilamoura.
Boat hire for deep-sea fishing trips for parties of up to 12.

HOTEL VIKING Praia Senhora da Rocha, 4 km west of Armação de Pêra.
Board hire and tuition, plus scuba-diving lessons. Explore the interesting underwater caves in the area.

CONJUNTO TURISTÍCO VILALARA Praia Redonda, 4 km west of Armação de Pêra, and just east of Senhora da Rocha.
Ski hire and lessons.

HOTEL ALFA MAR Praia da Falésia, 10 km east of Albufeira.
Board and ski hire and lessons.

CLUBE TORPEDO Aldeia do Mar, Vilamoura.
Equipment hire and scuba-diving lessons.

ESCOLA DE WINDSURF Praia de Faro, Faro.
Board hire and lessons. Perfect for beginners.

ALGARVE...E
Schweppes

Albufeira: Pop: 26,000. Tourist information: Rua 5 de Outubro, tel: 089-512144. The town takes its name – *al-Buhera* (castle on the sea) – from the Moors, who made it a stronghold. The white houses in the Old Town clearly show the Moorish influence. Badly damaged by earthquakes (see **A-Z**) in the 18thC (during which the medieval fortress was destroyed), in the early 1960s Albufeira began to flourish as a tourist centre, and is now the most popular resort on the coast. Visit the Capela de Misericórdia; originally built in the 16thC, it was modified and restored in the 19thC and has a fine example of a Manueline (see **A-Z**) doorway. You can reach the main beach by a tunnel under the Hotel Sol e Mar but don't ignore the smaller Fishermen's Beach. Both become crowded in the summer, and you may prefer the smaller coves at São Rafael (5 km west) or Olhos de Água (5 km east). The fishmarket is held daily (except Mon.) at a site just north of the town centre on the ring road towards Montechoro. The regional market is held on the road towards Armação de Pêra. See **ALBUFEIRA.**

Fishing boats on the beach at Albufeira

Armação de Pêra

Alte: 28 km northeast of Albufeira. This is one of the prettiest villages in the Algarve. Be sure to visit the Igreja Matriz, the local parish church. It has a 16thC Manueline (see **A-Z**) doorway and superb Manueline fonts, valuable 16thC Sevillan *azulejos* (see **A-Z**), and a magnificent retable in *talha dourada* (see **A-Z**). The springs which lie next to the village of Fonte Grande make an ideal setting for a picnic. See **FARO-EXCURSION 1**.

Armação de Pêra: 18 km west of Albufeira. A famous seaside resort which has grown up around a small fishing village and boasts what is claimed to be the longest beach in the Algarve. It is overlooked by the remains of an 18thC fortress. Take a boat to visit the caves of Pontal and Ruazes, carved into the cliffs by the sea. There is a wide range of hotels, restaurants, bars and discos in the area. See **ALBUFEIRA-EXCURSION, BEACHES 2**.

Azulejos: These are glazed earthenware tiles, reminders of the Moorish origins of much of the art and culture of this area. You can find them everywhere, on house walls, public fountains, garden benches, station walls and, above all, in churches. The best places in the Algarve to see *azulejos* are: Igreja São Lourenço, Almansil; Igreja Matriz, Alte ; Capela de Santo António, Lagos; Igreja de São Francisco and the Catedral, Faro; Igreja de Nossa Senhora da Conceição, Loulé; Igreja Santa Bárbara de Nexe; and the Palácio de Estói.

Barrocal: This is an area of the Algarve, lying between the Serra and the coast, which stretches from Silves to São Brás de Alportel, and from São Bartoloméu de Messines to Loulé. Essentially rural and agricultural, the Barrocal offers delightful countryside which is still virtually undiscovered by the tourists who gather on the beaches along the coast of the Algarve. See **FARO-EXCURSIONS 1 & 2**.

Bullfighting: Unlike the Spanish practice, bulls are not killed in Portuguese bullfights (*touradas*). The *tourada* begins with riders (*cavaleiros*) sticking banderillas (*farpas*) in the bull's neck. When the bull shows signs of exhaustion it is controlled by *forcados*, men armed with long forks. The overpowered bull is usually taken to the slaughterhouse the next morning. *Touradas* are held once or twice a week Easter-Oct. The performances are announced the week before in the local press and on signs in the streets.

Carvoeiro: 8 km east of Portimão. A village on one of the loveliest bays on the coast. From here you can take a boat along the coast to Armação de Pêra (see **A-Z**). This stretch of coastline has some of the least-known beaches in the Algarve: Vale de Centianes, Carvalho, Cabo Carvoeiro. There is also the charming village of Benagil, lying in a cove between Carvoeiro and Armação de Pêra, and the bay of Senhora da Rocha with its white chapel on the cliffs overlooking the beach and the cave. Before reaching the beach at Carvoeiro, a road leads off to the left to the underwater caves of the Algar Seco.

Carvoeiro

Sunset over the hills of the Serra near Castro Marim

Castro Marim: 52 km northeast of Faro. An ancient fortress town, Castro Marim is dominated by the ruins of a medieval castle (built in the 12thC) and by the walls of a 17thC fortress. The castle was badly damaged by the earthquake (see **A-Z**) in 1755, and it has been only partially restored (0900-1900 summer, 0900-1800 winter). From the castle there are beautiful views out over the Guadania estuary, the saltpans, the Sapal de Castro Marim nature reserve and the Serra. See **FARO-EXCURSION 2.**

Earthquake: On 1 Nov. 1755, while Portugal was celebrating All Saints' Day, a terrible earthquake devastated the country. The epicentre was not far off the coast of the Algarve. Lisbon was destroyed in about five minutes and buildings and monuments all over the country were destroyed, particularly in Sagres, Lagos, Silves and Faro.
As if that was not enough, a tidal wave caused by the earthquake hit the coast, causing catastrophic damage, and silting up the rivers and harbours. As a result of the earthquake, most of the buildings have been extensively restored, although some elements of their older appearance such as Manueline-style (see **A-Z**) doorways and *azulejos* (see **A-Z**) remain.

The cobbled streets of Estói

Estói & Milreu: 10 km north of Faro. Estói is well worth visiting for the Palácio de Estói. The palace is a superb 18thC mansion encrusted with extravagant (and kitsch) details. The house is private property but you can visit the gardens which have a formal, terraced layout and some *azulejos* (see **A-Z**). A mile away at Milreu are the ruins of a Roman villa which once housed a fine collection of mosaics, jewels, ornaments, statues and pottery. The collection is scattered among various museums in Lisbon, Faro and Lagos, and there is little now left here. See FARO-EXCURSION 2.

Fado: The songs of the Fado are the main feature of Portuguese folk music and may be melancholy or more upbeat. The sad songs, usually about unrequited love and sung by a woman with guitar accompaniment, have a haunting quality. These are the most famous kind of Fado songs, but so as not to send the audience home brokenhearted, some lighter, happier tunes will also be mixed in. Some artists are famous nationwide, and their appearances are eagerly anticipated, so make sure you book a table at the venues where they perform. For details of the nearest Fado performance look in one of the local listings magazines (see **What's On**).

Faro: Pop: 42,000. Tourist information: Rua da Misericórdia, tel: 089-803604. Although Faro is the regional capital of the Algarve and boasts good, varied attractions, it is less popular with tourists than the resorts along the coast. Of particular interest is the Old Town, entered by the main gate, Arco da Vila, which lies at the south end of the Manuel Bolivar gardens, next to the tourist office. Along Rua do Município is the Largo da Sé and the Catedral (Sé). The cathedral has been restored and it is difficult to trace its original early-Gothic style. It is decorated in a simple Renaissance manner and the walls are covered with beautiful 18thC *azulejos* (see **A-Z**). Inside, there are two interesting chapels: São Francisco de Paola and Nossa Senhora dos Prazeres (Our Lady of the Pleasures). Behind the cathedral is the Convento de Nossa Senhora da Assunção, which houses the Museu Arqueológico Infante Dom Henrique. The museum has a comprehensive collection of sculptures, jewels, earthenware, paintings and mosaics from Milreu (see **Estói &**

Milreu), and *azulejos* and semiprecious stones. The Igreja de São Francisco is an 18thC church with beautiful *azulejos,* and the Igreja Misericórdia has a fine Renaissance portal. The Museu Etnográfico Regional, with displays of all the regional crafts, is also worth visiting. The 18thC district, a much reconstructed area, stretches from the pedestrian Rua de Santo António to the Largo do Carmo. This district, known as A Baixa, is the centre of commercial and social life in Faro. There are some very fine buildings, houses and palaces in Rua de Santo António, Rua do Conselheiro Bivar, Rua do Lethes and Praça D. Marcelino Franco. The Igreja do Carmo, with its high towers, is the most impressive religious building in Faro. This is a Baroque church with a rich interior decorated with *talha dourada* (see **A-Z**) woodcarving. Don't leave without seeing the strange Capela dos Ossos, whose walls are covered with bones. See **FARO**.

Henry the Navigator (1394-1460): Son of King João I and Queen Philippa of Lancaster, Henry came to prominence when at the age of just 21 he successfully led the conquest of Ceuta. But aged 25, when Governor of Gibraltar and Master of the Straits, he withdrew to Sagres to dedicate himself to science, mysticism and the preparations necessary for the great discoveries of the 15thC – the voyages down the west coast of Africa, the discovery of India and the circumnavigation of the world. He gathered together a formidable team of geographers, cartographers, master mariners, astronomers and scientific instrument makers. His court became one of the most advanced and highly cultured of its time. He directed and encouraged the research which led to the drawing of the first maps of the Atlantic, to the improvement of astronomical navigation and also to the invention of the caravel, the light and manoeuvrable ship which would carry the Portuguese all round the world. He made Lagos the starting point for expeditions (Madeira 1419, Açores 1427, Cabo Bojador 1434) and used Sagres as an observatory, spending countless lonely hours on the rocky promontory gazing out into the Atlantic swells, contemplating the charting of new lands. By the time of his death the Portuguese were setting out on the maritime conquest of the world, made possible by his efforts and inspiration.

Praça da República, Lagos

Joanine Style: A Baroque style of decoration adapted to Portugal, it flourished at the end of the 17thC and lasted until the late 18thC under the reigns of kings João IV and João V. This was the era of very extravagant altars in carved and gilded wood (*talha dourada* – see **A-Z**) and of superb coloured *azulejos* (see **A-Z**) from Seville and Évora.

Lagos: Pop: 15,000. 18 km east of Portimão. Tourist information: Largo Marques de Pombal, tel: 082-763031. An important harbour town as early as the 14thC, and the capital of the Algarve from 1576 to 1756, the city lost a great deal of its influence as a result of the earthquake (see **A-Z**) of 1755. However, Lagos still has lots to offer its visitors – the famous Baroque chapel of Santo António, a charming museum and a maze of paved streets enclosed by walls and towers. The museum is small, nicely old-fashioned and has an eclectic collection of exhibits. Over the last few years tourism has developed considerably on the attractive neighbouring beaches of Meia Praia and Dona Ana (see **BEACHES 1**), but the city and its atmosphere have been largely preserved from the inroads of mass tourism. After walking round the Old Town you might wish to admire the sea views at Ponta da Piedade, a complex cliff formation, worn by the sea into swirling shapes and marine caves, which lies about 2 km south of Lagos (take the road to Sagres, turn left to Praia Dona Ana, then right until you reach the lighthouse). You can also sail to the cliffs, leaving from the small harbour beside the Forte da Pau da Bandeira. See **LAGOS**.

Loulé: 20 km northwest of Faro. Tourist information: Edifício do Castelo, tel: 089-63900. An important market town, Loulé's Muslim origins are still apparent. It is famous for the flower-covered floats of the carnival in Feb. or Mar., and the procession of Nossa Senhora da Piedade during Holy Week. The historical centre can be easily covered on foot. Gathered around the market you will find skilful craftsmen producing wickerwork, embroidery, pottery, *azulejos* (see **A-Z**), ironwork, leather goods, woodcarvings and copperwork (particularly the coppersmiths in Rua 9 de Abril). Visit the Gothic Igreja Matriz (13thC) with its Renaissance portal and richly decorated interior. There are superb *azulejos* in the Chapel of the Souls and Chapel of

Loulé

Consolation. From the church gardens there are views over the terraced roofs and chimneys of the city. The city walls are reminders of the old Arabic fortress, rebuilt in the 13thC. On Avenida Marçal Pacheco you can see the fine Manueline (see **A-Z**) portal of the Igreja da Misericórdia which also has a granite transept. At the opposite side of town is a monument dedicated to the memory of town planner Duarte Pacheco, Salazar's minister for civil engineering who died in a car crash in 1943. Two kilometres west towards Albufeira on the EN 270 you can stop at the Sanctuary of Nossa Senhora da Piedade with its Renaissance chapel. There is also a fine view of the countryside and the sea. See **FARO-EXCURSION 1**.

Manueline Style: Named after King Manuel I, crowned in 1495, the Manueline style shows very specific features. It broke with the traditional Gothic structure and made use of references to the great discoveries. Columns and capitals, doors, windows and vaults are covered in carved cables, ropes, rigging and anchors, and exotic flowers. The style, symbolizing the new prosperity of the country, disappeared as suddenly as it had arrived on the death of the king. The following are outstanding examples: the parish church in Alcantarilha; the red sandstone church of Alvor; the small church of Estômbar; the parish churches of Monchique and São Bartoloméu de Messines; the window of the Igreja da Misericórdia in Silves; and the side door of the Renaissance church in Luz de Tavira.

Moncarapacho: 8 km north of Olhão and 18 km east of Faro. A peaceful village on the slopes of the Cerro de São Miguel and the Cerro da Cabeça, Moncarapacho is surrounded by orchards full of almond and orange trees. Note also the parish church and its Renaissance doorway. See **FARO-EXCURSION 2**.

Monchique: 24 km north of Portimão. A small village with tiny houses lining the narrow streets. The parish church (*igreja matriz*) has a Manueline (see **A-Z**) porch. Walk up to the ruins of the Franciscan convent and enjoy the wide views over the Algarve. Nearby is the small village of Caldas de Monchique, the only spa in the Algarve. It is a charming, elegant place with a peaceful atmosphere. Although the thermal baths themselves are now a shopping centre, the spa water is sold in bottles. Just one sip of this foul-smelling water is supposed to prolong your life by ten years! See **LAGOS-EXCURSION 1**.

Olhão: 8 km east of Faro. A busy little fishing harbour, Olhão deserves a visit if only to climb the parish church tower on Praça da Restauração. The local priest will open it on request. From the top you can see what remains of the famous *açoteias*, the terraced roofs of the one-storey houses which are linked by a maze of corridors and steps. The walk back to the harbour will take you through picturesque streets – long rows of white, low-roofed houses, covered or lined with colourful earthenware tiles. From Easter to Oct. small boats run to the beaches on the opposite side of the *ria* (estuary) on the sand islands of Armona and Culatra (see **BEACHES 4**). See **FARO-EXCURSION 2**.

Portimão: Pop: 35,000. 18 km east of Lagos and 29 km west of Albufeira. Tourist information: Largo 1 de Dezembro, tel: 082-23695. An important sardine-fishing port on the west bank of the Arade estuary and the main trade centre in the western Algarve. The city was destroyed during the 1755 earthquake (see **A-Z**) and doesn't have much in the way of historical interest. You may want to spend a day here to go shopping in the pedestrianized streets, or to go swimming at Praia da Rocha (see **BEACHES 2**), the oldest resort in the Algarve. See **LAGOS-EXCURSION 1, PORTIMÃO**.

Quarteira: 22 km west of Faro and 26 km east of Albufeira. A fishing harbour and modern seaside resort stretching along a sandy beach between the tourist developments of Vale do Lobo and Vilamoura. The original village has been swamped by overdevelopment. There are no points of real interest other than the local market, the beach and the seafront bars and restaurants.

Sagres: 33 km west of Lagos. This is a small fishing harbour situated a few kilometres from the 'World's End' at Cabo de São Vicente. Sagres flourished during the time of Henry the Navigator (see **A-Z**) and he had

Sacred Promontory

a fortress built here, more for scientific purposes (an observatory) than for strategic ones. The city was raided by Sir Francis Drake, who destroyed what little remained of Henry's observatory.
The citadel is entered through a tunnel in the walls. Inside, though, there is little to evoke the past except a huge stone compass set into the compound floor and above, up the steps, a small sundial. A museum is currently under construction.
A visit to the Sacred Promontory is also recommended. Hercules was reputedly buried here and St. Vincent's corpse is said to have been washed ashore at the cape which carries his name. See **LAGOS-EXCURSION 2**.

Santa Bárbara de Nexe: 12 km northwest of Faro. A little village which boasts one of the Algarve's prettiest churches. Gothic in origin, inside are superb, and very rare, 17thC polychrome alabaster *azulejos* (see **A-Z**), along with a splendid *talha dourada* (see **A-Z**) altar. See **FARO-EXCURSION 1**.

São Brás de Alportel: 18 km north of Faro. A small market town on the edge of the Barrocal (see **A-Z**), home town of Ibn Ammar, the illustrious poet of the court of Silves, and at the heart of a rural area. All kinds of traditional craft industries are preserved here – choose from ceramics, leatherwork, basketry, woodcarving, cork or confectionery at the busy Sat. market. Don't miss the *talha dourada* (see **A-Z**) altar of the Capela do Senhor dos Passos (immediately on the right coming from Faro and in front of the town hall). See **FARO-EXCURSION 2**.

Silves: 17 km northeast of Portimão. Once the capital of the Arab kingdom in the area, Silves is now a peaceful town lying on the banks of the Arade, dominated by the walls of its fortress. Silves had its heyday from the 9thC to the 12thC. It was the seat of the Arab court (they called it Xelb) and a flourishing commercial and intellectual centre. During the recapture of the town in the 13thC the Crusaders razed all the mosques to the ground. Lagos became the regional capital, and the bishopric transferred to Faro in the 16thC. The final blow to the influence of Silves came with the 1755 earthquake (see **A-Z**) and the subsequent silting up of the Arade. Visit the red sandstone fortress (0900-1900, till 1800 in winter). There is a beautiful view from

Silves

the walls over the gardens inside and the extensive orchards of the surrounding area. In the square below the fortress stands the cathedral built (in red and white sandstone) immediately after the recapture of the town by the Christians. The cathedral has a choir in the Flamboyant style, and fine emblazoned tombs of the Crusaders who fell in capturing the town. You should not miss the Igreja da Misericórdia which lies in front of the cathedral and has a famous Manueline (see **A-Z**) window. See **ALBUFEIRA-EXCURSION**.

Talha Dourada: An artistic style which appeared at the beginning of the 17thC. It consists of elaborately carved and sculpted wood which is then gilded. Usually set above and around altars, especially during the Baroque period, it can give the impression that the church is streaming with gold. Many of the masterpieces are anonymous.

Tavira

Tavira: 29 km northeast of Faro. Tourist information: Praça da República, tel: 081-22511. Tavira is a pleasant town deserving at least a half-day visit. All through Tavira are town houses with fine classical façades (often decorated) which give the town a very aristocratic appearance. Now badly silted up, the harbour, used for tuna fishing, was the oldest and most important in the province.
Park on Praça da República beside the river and enter the Old Town by the steps in front of the tourist office. Visit the Igreja da Misericórdia (note the superb portal) and admire the carvings and 18thC *azulejos* (see **A-Z**). Further on is the Castelo dos Mouros (gardens: 0900-1700 Mon.-Thu., 1000-1800 Sat. & Sun.).
On top of the hill is the lovely Largo da Graça and the Gothic façade of the Igreja Santa Maria do Castelo which has *azulejos* in three of its naves. Turn back, following Rua Peres Correia down to Rua da Liberdade (the bridge across the river is of Roman origin). Keep to the right bank and after 2 km is the fishing port. From here you can sail to Ilha de Tavira or Cabanas on the opposite side of the estuary (see **BEACHES 4**). See **FARO-EXCURSION 2**.

Vila Real de Santo António: 53 km east of Faro. Designed by Pombal, King José I's premier and architect of the Reconstruction, it was built on the pattern of the Baixa district in Lisbon. The streets are lined up, straight as a die, along the left bank of the Guadiana estuary, opposite the Spanish town of Ayamonte. See the Praça Marquês de Pombal – beautiful classical façades round a square paved with black and white mosaics.
There is a small museum, the Galeria Nacional Manuel Cabanas, with collections of wood cuts and wood engravings (1400-2000, 2100-2300 summer, 1500-1900 winter; closed Tue. & hols). A ferry runs to Ayamonte every 30 min 0830-2030 or you can cross by the new bridge. From Vila Real you can also take a pleasure trip up the river to Castro Marim (see **A-Z**) and Alcoutim. Ask at the fishing harbour to arrange this and fix prices and times. West of Vila Real is Monte Gordo (see **BEACHES 4**), a resort with a casino. The beach is wide and backed with dunes and pine woods but the town itself has little of interest. See **FARO-EXCURSION 2**.

Accidents & Breakdowns: If you are involved in an accident, exchange insurance details with other parties and contact the police. You'll find SOS points every 3 km on main roads. On secondary roads you'll have to find a telephone and dial 115 (free call) for police, ambulance if needed, or the fire brigade, who will either tow your car away for you or give you the number of the nearest 24 hr garage. The ACP (Portuguese Automobile Club) provides free services for its members, and for associate members, in its own garages in Lagos, Portimão and Faro. Members should tel: 01-3563931. See **Consulates**, **Driving**, **Emergency Numbers**.

Accommodation: There are five different types of accommodation available in the Algarve. Hotels are classified from one to five stars. Most of the three-, four- and five-star hotels on the coast have swimming pools and/or private access to the beach. They will have rooms with telephones, television and air conditioning, and will often have sports facilities. Tourist villages (*aldeia turística*) consist of several different areas with villas, apartments or bungalows. There are usually also hotels, sports facilities, supermarkets, bars and restaurants. Inns (*estalgems*) are generally simpler than hotels of an equivalent category, and cheaper, but this does not always follow. *Pousadas* are State-run hotels often in historical buildings such as monasteries and castles. They are usually quiet, with only a few rooms. The food and service are excellent. Booking is advisable. There are two *pousadas* in the Algarve, one in São Brás de Alportel and one in Sagres. Both of these are modern, although the Sagres *pousada* offers annexe accommodation – the old Forte do Beliche (see **LAGOS-EXCURSION 2**). *Pensãos* and *residências*, rated from one to four stars, are small bed and breakfast hotels of varying standards and character. A good one is worth its weight in gold, providing far better value and character than an anonymous international hotel, but do check the room before agreeing to take it. See **Camping & Caravanning**, **Youth Hostels**.

Airport: The Algarve's international airport lies 7 km west of Faro (10 min by bus or car, and about 30 min from Albufeira). The bus to Faro costs 125 Esc. and the taxi about 900 Esc. Hotels and tour operators send their own minibuses to pick up holiday-makers on arrival. There is a tourist office in the arrival area which will help you with bookings, transport and tourist information. In the departure area are a bar, restaurant, newsstand and souvenir shop. For information, tel: airport, 089-818582; TAP, 089-818908; and BA, 089-818320.

Baby-sitters: Most of the hotels and tourist villages offer baby-sitting services. You can contact them through the reception office. During the summer it's best to book in advance. The service costs 1000-1600 Esc. per hr, increasing significantly after 2400. See **CHILDREN**, **Children**.

Banks: See **Currency**, **Money**, **Opening Times**.

Beaches: There is a wide variety of beaches: from the vast, deserted and wild beaches of Carrapateira (a surfer's paradise) to the safe family beaches at Faro; from the spectacular and cosmopolitan Praia da Rocha to the intimate coves around Albufeira; and from the wide expanse of sand and the pine woods of Monte Gordo to the quiet fishing beaches of Ferragudo or Salema. Most beaches have at least one restaurant and many provide facilities for a variety of water sports. See **BEACHES 1-4**.

Best Buys: There are many attractive souvenirs which also offer good value for money. Look out for wickerwork; *empreita* (basketwork made from dwarf palms); wrought iron (ranging from key holders to balconies); pottery and ceramics; sweaters and plaids made from local wool; lace made according to Madeirean patterns; and carved wood. Gold and silver filigree, though not an Algarvian speciality, is also a good buy. See PORTIMÃO-SHOPPING, **Markets**.

Bicycle Hire: Cycling is a pleasant way to explore the area you are staying in. Bikes can be rented by the hour, half day, day or week. You may need to pay in advance and you will have to leave a deposit or some form of identification. Ask at tourist offices or your hotel reception for details of the nearest hire shop.

Bird-watching: The Algarve is rich in birdlife and this guide covers areas of special interest to bird-watchers, in particular Castro Marim (see **A-Z**), and Ria Formosa (south of Faro), where many species are now protected. Some organizations arrange bird-watching trips by car. Contact the West Algarve Riding Centre, Quinta dos Amarjões, Burgau, tel: 082-69152.

Boats: A boat service from Vila Real de Santo António to Ayamonte in Spain operates 0830-2030. However, the new Guadiana bridge across the river is open 24 hr. There are boats from Faro out to its beaches, from Olhão to the islands of Culatra (see BEACHES 4) and Armona, and from Tavira to Ilha de Tavira (see BEACHES 4). Sightseeing boats take tourists up and down the coast on day and half-day trips, leaving from Carvoeiro, Armação de Pêra, Portimão, Sagres or Albufeira. Information is available from any tourist office.

Budget: 1992 prices

Accommodation (two people)	6000-25,000 Esc.
Lunch/dinner for two (exc. wine)	4000-9000 Esc.
Museum admission	200 Esc.
Coffee	100 Esc.
Brandy	500 Esc.
Beer (small)	100-150 Esc.
Short taxi ride	500 Esc.

Buses: The most convenient and cheapest way of travelling in the Algarve is by bus. Rodoviária Nacional (RN) has a very well-developed network which runs to all the main resorts and small villages. The buses are orange and white. You can consult timetables at any tourist office, bus station or hotel. For long-distance express buses (to Lisbon, for instance) you must book a seat through a travel agent, but for local buses tickets can be bought on board.

Cameras & Photography: All the main brands of film are available at photography shops, newsstands and sometimes in souvenir shops. Developing usually takes 24 hr, although you can find express services (which take 1 hr and may be of lower quality) in the main tourist centres.

Camping & Caravanning: Camp sites are usually situated along the coast, close to beaches. Some of them are very good value, well laid-out, with plenty of sports facilities and good sanitation. The Portuguese National Tourist Office (see **Tourist Information**) publishes an annual leaflet listing all the camp sites in the Algarve. It is advisable to have a camping carnet, obtainable from the Camping Club, tel: 0203-694995, or Federação Portuguesa de Campismo, Rua Voz de Operário 1, Lisbon 1000.

Car Hire: The main agencies have branches at the international airport in Faro and in the main towns (Lagos, Portimão, Albufeira, Faro, Tavira and Vila Real de Santo António). To hire a car you must be over 23 and have a driving licence issued more than a year previously. If your credit card is not accepted you will have to leave a deposit. The charges you will be quoted will include third-party insurance but not the government tax, which will be added to your bill. The rental agencies at Faro airport include: Hertz, tel: 089-818357; Avis, tel: 089-818395; and Guerin, tel: 089-818222. See **Driving**.

Chemists: *Farmácias* are open 0900-1300, 1500-1900 Mon.-Fri., 0900-1300 Sat. There is also usually a chemist on duty through the night. Addresses are posted in the windows and in newspapers. You may be charged 10% extra for this service. See **Health**.

Children: In most tourist centres hotels and holiday clubs vie with one another to keep children busy. Beach contests and sports competitions are organized throughout the season and playgrounds are available for smaller children on many popular beaches. Check with the reception staff of your hotel or holiday complex for programmes, schedules, tuition costs and locations of activities. Children under eight get a hotel discount of 50% if they share a room with their parents. See CHILDREN.

Climate: The Algarve's climate is half Mediterranean, half Atlantic: neither too hot (rarely above 30°C) in the summer, nor too cold in the winter (10°C is usually the coldest it gets). The average rainfall is low and there are over 300 days of sunshine a year. The water temperature stays around 21-22°C in summer and around 15-17°C Nov.-Mar.

Complaints: If you have been overcharged, or have a complaint about a hotel, restaurant or other establishment, ask to see the owner or manager of the premises. If he or she is unable to settle the matter to your satisfaction, ask for the complaints book which by law all establishments dealing with tourists must keep. One copy of the complaint form is retained by you, and another is sent to the tourist board and is signed as acknowledgment. You may find that just threatening this course of action will produce the desired effect. Alternatively, seek further advice from the nearest tourist office or the police.

Consulates:
UK – Rua de Estrela 4, Lisbon 1200, tel: 01-3954082.
UK – Largo Francisco Mauricio 7, Portimão 8500, tel: 082-417800.
Australia – Avenida da Liberdade 244-4, Lisbon, tel: 01-523350.
USA – Avenida das Forças Armadas, Lisbon 1600, tel: 01-7266600.

Conversion Chart:

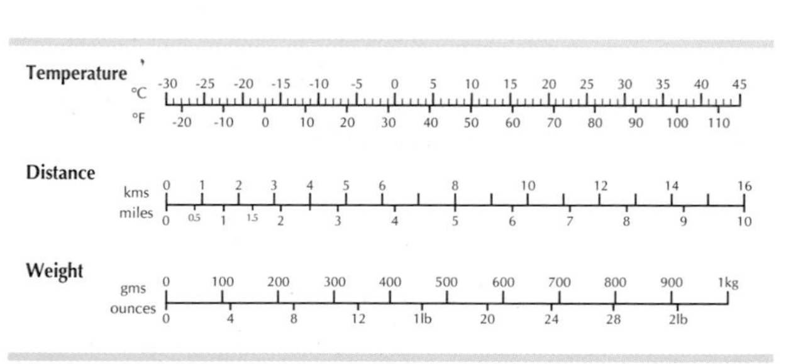

Credit Cards: See **Money**.

Crime & Theft: It is vital that you report loss or theft of passports, money, traveller's cheques, etc. to the nearest police station immediately. Make sure you obtain a copy of the police report for submission with your insurance claim. While most local people are honest, you are advised to deposit valuables in the hotel safe and not to leave anything in your car. Theft from hire cars is now quite common on the Algarve.

Currency: The Portuguese monetary unit is the escudo (Esc.), divided into 100 centavos.
Coins – 2.5, 5, 10, 20, 50, 100 and 200 Esc.
Notes – 500, 1000 and 10,000 Esc.
See **Money**.

Customs Allowances:

UK/EC	Cigarettes	Cigarillos	Cigars	Tobacco	Still Table Wine	Spirits/Liqueurs	Fortified Wine	Additional Still Table Wine	Perfume	Toilet Water	Gifts & Souvenirs
Duty Free	200	100	50	250 g	2 l	1 l	2 l	2 l	60 cc/ml	250 cc/ml	£32
Duty Paid	800	400	200	1 kg	90 l*	10 l	20 l				

(or) between Cigarettes, Cigarillos, Cigars and Tobacco; (or) between Spirits/Liqueurs, Fortified Wine and Additional Still Table Wine.

* Of which no more than 60 l should be sparkling wine.

Since 1 Jan. 1993 restrictions on allowances for duty-paid goods brought into the UK from any EC country have been abolished. Travellers are now able to buy goods, including alcoholic drinks and tobacco, paying duty and VAT in the EC country where the goods are purchased. However, duty-paid goods should be for the traveller's own use and carried by him personally. Whereas previously there were either-or options, travellers can now bring back the sum of the goods in the duty-paid column.

Disabled People: The Portuguese National Tourist Office (see **Tourist Information**) has a list of hotels that claim to provide access to wheelchair users. RADAR, 25 Mortimer St, London W1N 8AB, tel: 071-6375400, publishes *Holidays and Travel Abroad – A Disabled Guide,* covering Portugal and the Algarve. Another good source of information in the UK is the Holiday Care Service, tel: 0293-774535. It is also worth remembering that wheelchairs can be hired from *centros de enfermagem* (nursing centres) in most towns in the Algarve. See **Health**, **Insurance**.

Drinks: Local table wines are cheap and usually of a good standard. Ask for the *vinho da casa*, the house wine; *tinto* is red, and *branco* is white. Local wines include Dão Terras Altas (rich and full bodied), Periquita (fruity), Reguengos de Monsarraz (robust), Colares (light and

fruity) and Tavira (a common Algarvian wine). *Vinho verde* (green wine) is so called because it is made from early-picked grapes and drunk young. For dessert wines, try Moscatel de Setúbal, Lagoa or Carcavelos. There are also the sparkling rosé wines (Mateus and Raposeira) and, of course, port and Madeira. Spirits produced locally include: Medronho, made from berries (very strong); Bagaço, a fiery distillation akin to marc or grappa; Brandymel (brandy flavoured with honey); and Amêndoa Amarga, a sweet almond liqueur. Local beers are Sagres, Cristal and Super Bock. Coffee comes in a variety of forms: *uma bica* (small and black); *um garoto* (the same but with a drop of milk); *um galão* (larger and usually served in a glass); and *uma carioca* (water-diluted black coffee – American-style).

Driving: The national highway, the EN 125, which runs the length of the Algarve, is well maintained from Vila Real to Lagos, and beyond that major road-building work is in progress. Secondary roads are also quite well kept but should be driven with care. Safety belts are compulsory outside built-up areas and children under 13 must sit in the back. Traffic from the right normally has priority. The alcohol limit is 0.5 g per litre of blood. You can be fined if you exceed this limit. Speed limits are: 120 kph on highways, 90 kph on ordinary roads and 60 kph in built-up areas. Third-party insurance is required for drivers, so you will need a green card, obtainable from your travel company, the AA or RAC. In Portugal contact the Automóvel Clube de Portugal, Rua R. Araújo 24, Lisbon. Watch out for flocks of sheep, stray dogs, donkeys and carts, and careless Portuguese drivers who boast one of Europe's worst traffic accident records. See **Accidents & Breakdowns**, **Petrol**.

Drugs: The sale, possession or use of drugs is illegal. Contact your embassy or consulate (see **A-Z**) if you are arrested for a drugs-related offence, or the nearest hospital if you need medical help.

Eating Out: There are basically two types of restaurant in the Algarve. Snack bars serve drinks, salads, sandwiches, and some grilled meat or fish dishes at lunchtime. Their prices range from cheap to expensive depending on their location (facing the sea or on a main square they will be expensive). Restaurants range from family-run dining rooms serving simple local food to sophisticated places offering north European-orientated dishes (usually more expensive).
Breakfast (*pequeno almoço*) is usually served 0700-1000, lunch (*almoço*) 1200-1500, and dinner (*jantar*) 1930-2200. If you feel like something to eat after 2200, snack bars (*cervejaria*) usually stay open until 2400 or even 0200. Booking is advisable in the more fashionable restaurants in high season (mid July-mid Aug.).
Restaurants are officially ranked in four categories, from de luxe to third

class, but the quality of the food is not necessarily linked to this ranking, and you may enjoy a superb meal in a small, plain, local establishment. Fast-food places are plentiful in the modern tourist centres such as Quarteira and Albufeira. Beaches have at least one snack bar offering salads, sandwiches, etc. for lunch.
On the **RESTAURANTS** topic pages of this guide an Inexpensive meal would cost 4000-6000 Esc., a Moderate meal 5000-7000 Esc. and an Expensive meal 6000-9000 Esc. See the **RESTAURANTS** topic pages for **ALBUFEIRA**, **FARO**, **LAGOS** and **PORTIMÃO**, **Food**.

Electricity: The Algarve has a 220 V network. If you come from the USA or Canada you will need a plug adapter and a transformer.

Emergency Numbers: To call the police, an ambulance or the fire brigade dial 115 and the operator will connect you.
Police (non-emergency):
Albufeira, tel: 512205; Faro, tel: 803444; Portimão, tel: 417217; Quarteira, tel: 315662.

Events:
February-March: Carnival Week (week before Lent), pageants, processions, flower-covered floats, etc. Especially good in Loulé.
March-April: The Romaria da Senhora da Piedade is an important Easter Sun. procession at Loulé.
May-June: The Algarve Music Festival. Concerts are held in churches and theatres in Lagos, Faro, Portimão and Tavira. On 1 May there is a lively feast in the picturesque village of Alte.
Mid-July: Feste e Feira da Senhora do Carmo, an agricultural fair and show in Faro.
July-August: Summer Festival in Silves. Music, ballet and theatre in the ancient capital town.
September: National Folklore Festival. Traditional dances, music and songs in venues throughout the region.
October: Feira de Santa Iria, a large-scale traditional fair in Faro lasting several days; Feira de Outubro, a two-day fair in Monchique.
In summer many villages and seaside resorts organize fishing or folklore festivals, parish feasts and sports galas (tennis in Vilamoura, windsurfing in Praia da Rocha). For more details of all events, contact the local tourist office.

Excursions: Seville is only a 4 hr drive from Faro – Lisbon is 5 hr – and on the other side of the Serra is the attractive province of Alentejo, which is often ignored by visitors to the Algarve. If you are staying in the Algarve for more than a couple of weeks, take a two- or three-day round trip to the superb city of Évora. Travel agents arrange trips to Spain or Lisbon; you will find their leaflets at hotel reception desks or ask at the local tourist office. See **ALBUFEIRA-EXCURSION, FARO-EXCURSIONS 1 & 2, LAGOS-EXCURSIONS 1 & 2.**

Fishing: The Algarve is a paradise for fishermen, whether river anglers or deep-sea fishermen. A day aboard a fully-equipped big game fishing boat costs about 11,000 Esc. per fisherman. For more information, contact Clube de Amadores de Pesca, Rua do Salitre 175, Lisbon 1200. Though fishing seasons vary slightly from year to year and area to area, Mar.-July is the best time to fish for salmon and trout in the well-stocked lakes and rivers.

Castelejo

Food: Portuguese food is fresh and wholesome. Local dishes are *canja de galinha,* a rice and chicken broth, and *açorda de marisco,* fish and seafood soup with garlic bread and whipped eggs.
Fish and seafood are always fresh and usually priced per kilo, not per portion. Such dishes include: *sardinha grelhada,* sardines grilled over charcoal; *arroz de marisco,* rice cooked in a casserole with shellfish and spices; *caldeirada de peixe,* fish, shellfish, potatoes, tomatoes and onions stewed together; *bacalhau,* salted cod steak, often served *à brás* – a casserole with potatoes, onions and eggs; and *bife de atum,* tuna fish steak.

Meat and regional dishes include: *ameijoas na cataplana*, pork, baby clams, sausage, bacon, onions, peppers, garlic, parsley and white wine all cooked together in a casserole; *coelho assado*, roasted rabbit with onions, white wine and spices; *espetada mista*, beef, lamb and pork cubes on a skewer; *frango (de churrasco) piri piri*, grilled chicken in a hot spicy sauce; *cabrito estufado*, braised kid with onions, tomatoes and green peas; and *feijoada*, hotpot with pork, white beans, sausage and cabbage.
Local cheeses are: *Serra da Estrêla* or *Queijo da Serra*, a cheese made from ewe's milk; and *Queijo Fresco*, white and creamy fresh cheese.
Sweets and cakes are usually made from figs, almonds and eggs, mixed, dried or cooked in as many ways and shapes as possible.
Traditional desserts are *pudim Molotov*, a rich cocktail of meringue and caramel, crème caramel or *arroz doce*, rice pudding with cinnamon and cream.

Guides: A good selection of guided tours can be arranged by travel agents. However, there is no independent guide service for the Algarve as a whole.

Health: The main cities have hospitals with staff who speak foreign languages. The general English-speaking hospital is the Clínica do Monte Carvoeiro, tel: 082-357720. Obtain an E111 certificate from the DSS and produce it if you require treatment. Treatment is free at official hospitals but prescribed medicines and dental treatment has to be paid for. Keep all receipts for insurance claims. Inoculations are not required except for visitors arriving from epidemic areas. Tap water is drinkable everywhere in the Algarve.

Insurance: You should take out travel insurance covering you against theft and loss of property and money, as well as medical expenses, for the duration of your stay. Your travel agent should be able to recommend a suitable policy. See **Crime & Theft**, **Driving**, **Health**.

Laundries: Launderettes (*lavandarias*) are rare in the Algarve but you should find that most hotels provide a regular dry-cleaning service (2-3 days) and an express service (24 hr), though this will attract a supplementary charge.

Olhão

Lost Property: There is no central lost property office. Each service (buses, railways, etc.) has its own lost and found office. Contact the authorities at the terminal or the nearest police station.

Markets: Fresh fruit and vegetables from farms in the surrounding districts can be purchased at markets held 0800-1300 Mon.-Sat. in the market buildings in Albufeira, Lagos, Loulé, Portimão, Armação de Pêra and Vila Real de Santo António. Larger markets where you can buy clothes, shoes and handicrafts are held on the following days: Albufeira – 1st and 3rd Tue. of month; Almansil – 1st Sun. of month; Lagos – 1st Sat. of month; Loulé – every Sat.; Portimão – 1st Mon. of month; Quarteira – every Wed.; Silves – 3rd Mon. of month. See **Best Buys**.

Money: Major credit cards are accepted at airports, for car hire, in hotels, garages, and in large shops and restaurants. Your hotel will change money and may be cheaper than the banks. Don't forget your passport when changing traveller's cheques. See **Currency**, **Opening Times**.

Music: A few concerts are held during the summer in Faro's cathedral. Some of the main nightspots, as well as the casinos, feature performing artists during the summer. Check at the venue or in the local press. Rock music is inescapable, pouring out of the bars and beach restaurants. See **Fado**, **Nightlife**.

Newspapers: The main European titles are available the same day as publication. See **What's On**.

Nightlife: In the cosmopolitan tourist centres, such as Albufeira and Lagos, bars and nightclubs are plentiful, so you will have no trouble having an enjoyable night out. Entry to discos usually costs about 1000 Esc., which also entitles you to one free drink. There are three casinos in the Algarve, at Monte Gordo, Vilamoura and Praia da Rocha. Passports are required for entry into the gambling rooms and you must be over 21. Most large hotels provide nightly entertainment which is open to nonresidents. See **ALBUFEIRA-NIGHTLIFE, FARO-NIGHTLIFE, LAGOS-NIGHTLIFE.**

Opening Times:
Banks – 0830-1500 Mon.-Fri.
Shops – 0900-1300, 1500-1900 Mon.-Fri., 0900-1300 Sat. Shopping centres and supermarkets open 1000-2300.
Offices – 0900-1300, 1500-1900 Mon.-Fri.
Bars – 1100-0200.
Discos – 2200-0400/dawn.

Orientation: *Algarve 1:100,000* (Hildebrand's Travel Maps) gives more detail than most maps of the Algarve, though smaller roads and their numbers are not marked. It also has town plans of Albufeira, Faro, Lagos and Portimão. Place names and spellings vary from map to map. A few words worth knowing are: square – *praça, largo* or *campo*; beach – *praia*; church – *igreja* (parish church – *igreja matriz*).

Passports & Customs: A valid passport (or identity card for some EC visitors) is necessary, but no visa is required for stays of less than three months. There is no limit on the amount of money that can be brought in or out of the country. See **Customs Allowances**.

Petrol: Sold in litres and available in Super (four star) and Normal (two star). Unleaded petrol is also available. It is illegal to carry petrol in cans in the car. You'll have no problems finding petrol at night and at weekends. However, if you are planning a journey north into the countryside, bear in mind that petrol stations are scarce in the more remote areas. See **Driving**.

Police: A policeman wearing an armband marked 'CD' should be able to assist tourists and speak at least one foreign language. City policemen wear blue and rural policemen brown. The Guardia Nacional de República watches over the highways, carrying out document- and speed-checks. See **Crime & Theft**, **Emergency Numbers**.

Quarteira

Post Offices: *Correios Telégrafos e Telefones* (CTT). Offices in major towns open 0900-1900 Mon.-Fri. In Faro and Portimão the central post office opens on Sat. until 1230. Offices in smaller towns and villages open 0900-1230 and 1400-1800. You can have mail sent to you Posta Restante in the town of your choice, but don't forget your passport when you go to collect it. Stamps are available at newsstands and tobacconists. Postcards and letters to EC countries cost 65 Esc., and 120 Esc. for outside Europe.

Public Holidays: 1 Jan., Shrove Tue., Good Fri., 25 April, 1 May, Corpus Christi, 10 June (death of Camões and National Day), 15 Aug., 5 Oct., 1 Nov., 1 Dec., 8 Dec. and 25 Dec.

Rabies: Still exists in Portugal. As a precaution have all animal bites treated immediately by a doctor.

Railways: Operated by Caminhos de Ferro Portugueses. A railway service links Lagos to Vila Real de Santo António, serving the main points of the coast and more or less following the route of the EN 125. The stations are sometimes far from the city centre, as at Albufeira and Loulé, requiring a taxi or bus trip out. Trains are not very fast but quite frequent and they travel through much more interesting countryside than the road. On the Algarve routes, trains have first- and second-class cars but there is no restaurant car. Express trains take 4 hr to reach Lisbon from Faro or Portimão, with a change at the small junction of Tunes. Interrail, Eurorail and Transalpino passes can be used on the Portuguese network. CFP issues half-fare tickets for children under 12 and people over 65. Check at tourist offices for details.

Religious Services: Portugal is predominantly Roman Catholic. Masses are held every morning in parish churches. Services for other denominations are listed in the fortnightly *Algarve News* or you can ask at the nearest tourist office. Anglican, Baptist, Evangelist and Dutch Protestant services are all available.

Shopping: See PORTIMÃO-SHOPPING, **Best Buys**, **Markets**.

Smoking: Smoking is not allowed on city buses, in sports grounds and in cinemas or theatres. You may smoke on buses only in the last three rows and only on trips taking longer than 1 hr.

Sports: Apart from downhill skiing there are very few sports you can't enjoy in the Algarve. One of the top destinations for golfers from all over the world, the province also offers a wide variety of water sports at many well-equipped beaches. Each large hotel or tourist centre has tennis courts, bicycle hire and fitness centres, and you can usually hire windsurfing boards, sail or motorboats, water-skis and scuba-diving equipment. You can also have windsurfing, sailing, water-skiing or scuba-diving tuition at schools on the main beaches. They will give group or private lessons. Boats can be hired at the Marina de Vilamoura, one of the best marinas in Europe, with all kinds of services for sailors: repairs, dry docks, chandlers, etc. There are golf and tennis competitions throughout the year and other events, local, national or

international, too numerous to mention. Check with local tourist offices for up-to-the minute information. See **GOLF**, **HORSE RIDING**, **TENNIS**, **WATER SPORTS**.

The golf course at Quinta do Lago

Taxis: Cabs are black with green roofs. Cabs cannot be flagged down in the street; you must either book one through your hotel or wait at a taxi rank. Fares start with a flat charge of 200 Esc. plus 56 Esc. per km. This increases by 20% at weekends and after 2230. See **Tipping**.

Telephones & Telegrams: Public telephones: Crediphone booths accept a prepaid credit card which can be bought in post offices or shops. They come in units of 50 or 120. They are convenient for long-distance calls and can be found in most tourist areas. Coin-operated booths are found all over. They accept 10 and 20 Esc. coins and can be used for local and long-distance calls but are impractical for international calls because of the number of coins needed. Go instead to the post office, where you will be able to use a booth which is monitored, and pay the cashier afterwards. Hotels levy heavy charges on telephone bills. However, rates are reduced after 2000.

Codes: Dial 00 then the country code. For assistance dial 090 (national calls), 099 (European calls) or 098 (other countries).
You can send telegrams through the post office, your hotel or by dialling 183. Telegrams to European countries cost 950 Esc. plus 39 Esc. per word. See **Emergency Numbers**.

Television & Radio: There are two national TV channels, both of which show undubbed films. Large hotels and many bars also have satellite television. See the *Algarve Resident* for a weekly programme listing. You can receive European international broadcasts and Voice of America on short wave.
The Algarve's English-language radio stations are:
Solar Rádio – 90.5 FM/stereo (news at 0830, 1030, 1330 & 2030).
Rádio Clube de Sul – 101.6 FM/stereo.
Kiss FM – 101.2 FM/stereo.
Rádio Restauração – 102.3 FM (0900-1000 Sun.).
Rádio Atlantico – 104 FM (2100-2300 Sat. & Sun.; news at 0900, 1300 & 1900 Mon.-Fri.).

Time Difference: Portugal is on the Greenwich meridian and there is no time difference with the UK in summer. In winter it is 1 hr ahead.

Tipping: A service charge is usually included in the bill at hotels and restaurants. Tipping is not compulsory but you can add up to 10% to your bill if you appreciated the service. Tip taxi drivers, hairdressers, etc. on the same basis.

Toilets: The standard of hygiene in lavatories – *homens* (men), *senhoras* (women) – is reasonable. You may find a public convenience in a large town centre (it is customary to give the attendant a couple of coins). Otherwise, try using the facilities of a café, restaurant or hotel. You will never be challenged in a large hotel but do buy a drink in a café for courtesy's sake.

Tourist Information: Contact the Portuguese National Tourist Office, 22-25a Sackville St, London, W1X 1DE, tel: 071-4941441, for

Carvoeiro

information before you depart for the Algarve. The staff in the London office are helpful but only have limited information and will refer you to local offices on the Algarve. For tourist office addresses see the appropriate town entry in the cultural/historical gazetteer.

What's On: Four helpful English-language publications which give the latest details of what's on are: *Discover* (Portimão/Albufeira/Eastern Algarve), a free monthly magazine; *Algarve Gazette*, another monthly magazine; *Algarve Resident*, a weekly newspaper/magazine; and *Algarve News*, a fortnightly newspaper. A leaflet detailing the month's forthcoming events is also available from tourist offices. See **Events**.

Youth Hostels: You can stay in youth hostels in Portugal if you are aged 12-45 and have an international membership card. Those who do not have the card should be able to obtain it at the youth hostels themselves. There are two official youth hostels in the Algarve at Lugar da Coca Maravilhas, Portimão, tel: 082-85704, and Rua Dr Sousa Martins 40, Vila Real de Santo António, tel: 081-44565. Expect to pay 800-1350 Esc. per person per night. For more information, contact Pousadas de Juventude, Rua Andrade Corvo 46, Lisbon 1000, tel: 01-571054/522002.

Vila Real de Santo António

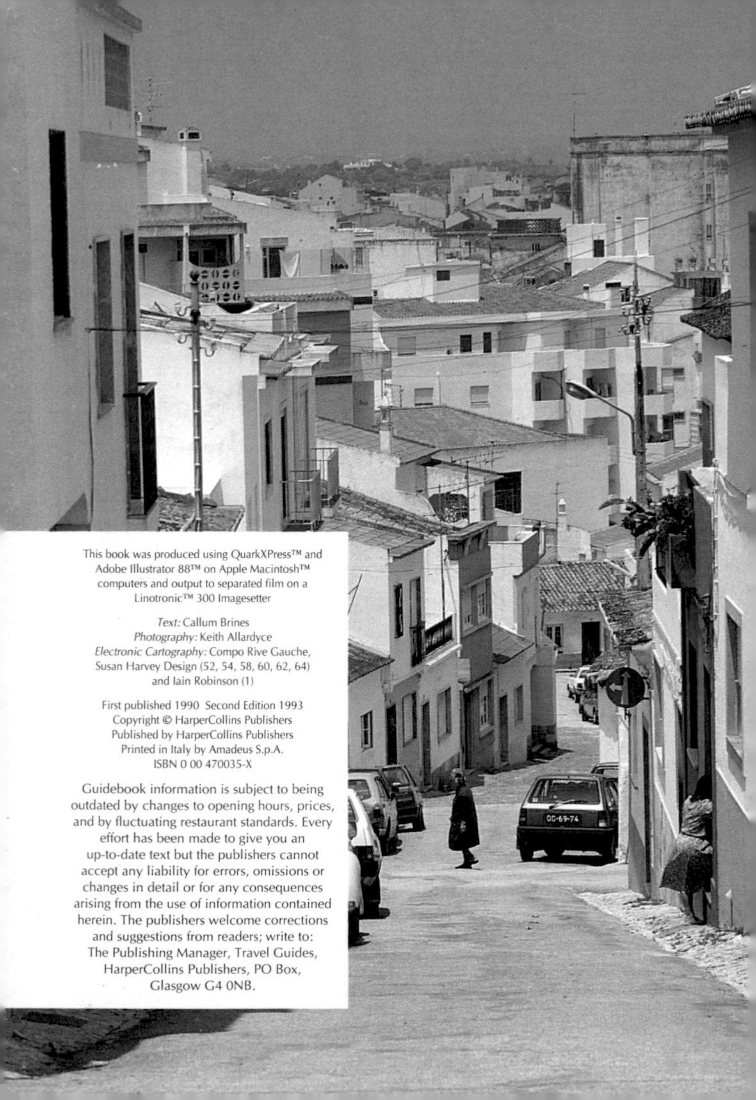

This book was produced using QuarkXPress™ and Adobe Illustrator 88™ on Apple Macintosh™ computers and output to separated film on a Linotronic™ 300 Imagesetter

Text: Callum Brines
Photography: Keith Allardyce
Electronic Cartography: Compo Rive Gauche, Susan Harvey Design (52, 54, 58, 60, 62, 64) and Iain Robinson (1)

First published 1990 Second Edition 1993

Published by HarperCollins Publishers
Printed in Italy by Amadeus S.p.A.
ISBN 0 00 470035-X

Guidebook information is subject to being outdated by changes to opening hours, prices, and by fluctuating restaurant standards. Every effort has been made to give you an up-to-date text but the publishers cannot accept any liability for errors, omissions or changes in detail or for any consequences arising from the use of information contained herein. The publishers welcome corrections and suggestions from readers; write to: The Publishing Manager, Travel Guides, HarperCollins Publishers, PO Box, Glasgow G4 0NB.